Learning to Walk With GOD

By

Dwight Hall
with
Cari Haus

Printed By

Remnant Publications
Coldwater, MI

Learning To Walk With God

This edition published 2002

Cover Design by Penny Hall

Cover Photos by Photo Disc

All Bible verses taken from the King James version
unless otherwise noted.

ISBN 1-883012-95-3

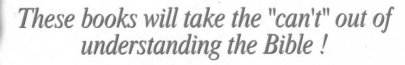

Contents

Dedication

First and foremost, I thank God for His love and mercy. I have dedicated this book to Him. Secondly to my parents, for without their love and guidance this book would not have been written. Thirdly, to my family, who had faith in me and allowed me to bear our testimony. Finally, to you the reader, that you may glean insights from the principles in this book, be encouraged and make a decision to walk that walk with God.

Forward

I listened eagerly, hopefully, as my eyes lingered over the pristine view from the pass. The Tobacco Valley below was still green and without snow, although in the pass where I stood, the snow was more than knee deep.

"Tom!" Dwight!" I yelled again, but there was no answer and my words merely melted into the snow, just as the sound of my horn had, a half a mile below where I had gotten stuck on my side of the range.

I had hoped they would be here waiting for me. I was supposed to meet Dwight's family at the summit which is halfway between my house and Tom's, but now as I stood there on that wind swept pass, I had no idea if they had gotten stuck, had turned back, or if they had run into some kind of trouble. So I turned toward the valley below and began to walk down the steep decent on their side, my mind reviewing the events that had brought me to this place.

I first had met Dwight when he was visiting Tom at the real-estate office where we both worked. He and Tom were old school friends and after renewing their acquaintance and seeing what we had gained in the mountains, he was very enthusiastic about bringing his family out to visit both of our families.

I had been a success by worldly standards. I had run a prospering business in the mid-west, but somehow, amid all that I had achieved, I found myself deeply troubled by my inability to form the type of deeply intimate relationships I longed for with my wife and children, not to mention my failure to find a Spiritual life that was more than just a form.

Perhaps I am not that unusual in those problems, but my response to that situation was. We sold the business, the fancy home, the extra vehicles and moved seventeen hundred miles away to the Montana wilderness determined to find the things in life that matter more than money. Now we had lived in the wilderness for a number of years and had found time to heal our marriage, time to truly be a family and the ability to really live each day with God as our leader. This had so satisfied us that no monetary success could entice us away.

Now I was supposed to spend some days with Dwight, another successful businessman. I knew we'd relate well, but how do you condense the lessons learned from years of hard experience into a few hours of conversation? Just in today's trip to meet him and his family I had found myself fighting what has become the most familiar battle of my life—the battle I fight against myself. You see, when my truck got bogged down in the deep snow my first inclination is to put on the chains and force my way higher and I had even gotten out of my vehicle to do just that, but something stopped me. I have learned that God truly does speak to us in the quiet recesses of our minds and the distinct impression I had was to leave the truck where it was and walk over the pass to meet Tom and Dwight. I found them about a half mile below the pass—also stuck in the snow. "We'll have to walk it from here." I told them, knowing I would soon receive an interesting revelation of their characters. To walk back the route I had taken was mostly uphill, a jaunt of more than a mile in deep and unbroken snow. It would be enough to test the mettle of anyone and most people used to the softer life of the civilization would find themselves complaining about the situation before they had gone very far.

Yet Dwight's family surprised me. They never complained. His wife looked happy and even smiled. The children adopted her attitude and I thought, "I think I'm going to enjoy this family."

"What do you hope to gain from our time together?" I asked Dwight.

"Jim, we are looking for a closer walk with God. We are looking to know God in the same way you came to know Him when you moved out here." I smiled for I understood his feelings exactly.

When my truck came into view, I gasped at what I saw. A large tree had fallen across the road just in front of my vehicle, missing it by just a few inches, but it wasn't just the near miss that took my breath away. No, it was the knowledge that the God I love and serve had told me not to try and move higher up the mountain and now I knew why. As I shared with Dwight and his family what had transpired on the way to meet them, the real impact of what had happened became clear. "Dwight," I concluded, "if I hadn't listened to God's impression in my thoughts and had chosen to do it my way, we would really be in trouble. This is truly a wilderness area and it's rare that anyone comes up here, even in the summer. Tom has long since gone back to his own home by now, so we would have had to walk out to civilization some twenty plus miles away." All of us joined in a prayer of gratitude and while I didn't know it then, this was to mark the beginning of many years of friendship between us.

It is important that God's people encourage each other and the testimony of how God has worked in our own lives is one of the best forms of encouragement there is. Therefore, I am delighted to recommend Dwight's story, *Learning to Walk With God*. Through his story, the great truths of the gospel are revealed and while there may be other ways to understand or explain these truths, there can be no doubt that God has worked in Dwight's life.

A prayerful reading of Dwight's book will fill the reader with the desire to know God better and leave them with a better understanding of how our Loving Father uses different experiences and different methods to reach each of us as individuals. May God bless each of you as you read.

Jim Hohnberger
Co-founder, Restoration International Inc.
Author of: *Escape To God*
     Empowered Living
     It's About People

1

Growing Up "Different"

Being different from everybody else is not easy. I know, because I was often the "odd man out" in public school.

"Dwight, are you coming to the school picnic tomorrow?" my friends would ask.

"I wish I could," I would reply. "But it's on Saturday, so I can't. Remember? That's the day my family goes to church."

"Oh yeah," they would say. But that did not stop me from hearing all about it before and after the picnic.

"Dwight, are you coming to the football game?"

"Dwight, are you coming to the track meet?"

"I wish you could come to my birthday party, Dwight."

The list of questions rolled on and on, and so many times I had to say, "I'm sorry I can't do that, because it's on my Sabbath."

I had a hard time explaining the Sabbath, too.

"A-hem. This may sound a little weird, but from sunset Friday to sunset Saturday, we don't do the things we normally do during the week."

"So what do you do on Saturdays?" my friends would ask. Many of them thought I went straight home after church to stare at the wall, bored stiff, until sundown.

I wish I could say I understood the Sabbath at that point in my life—that I knew how to keep it and why it was so important. I did love God and wanted to do what was right, but I did not have a living, moment-by-moment connection with Him. I learned all about the "dos" and the "don'ts" without really understanding the "whys." I did not understand that God's laws were for my well-being and happiness. That God set me apart to protect me from the harmful results of disobedience.

"There sure are a lot of rules," I grumbled every other day, with peer pressure rubbing it in. Many times I wished I could fit in better. I wanted so badly to be like my friends, and wished with all my heart that this whole problem of "being different" would just go away.

The differences in my lifestyle were evident during the regular school day as well. I remember standing in line with my hot lunch token one day, realizing that the menu items were ham sandwiches and beans with pork.

"Can't eat this, can't eat that," I mumbled to myself as I put cookies and applesauce—the only things I could eat—on my tray.

"What's the matter, Dwight," my friends wanted to know. "You're not hungry?" This happened many times, and although I told my friends I wasn't really hungry, inside I was ravenous.

Teachers noticed my "strange" eating habits too, of course. One even took the time to set me straight publicly.

"Dwight," she said in front of the whole class, "I know you don't eat pork. And it's true that pigs were unclean at one time because everyone fed them their garbage. But today it's OK to eat pork, because they feed pigs grain and corn."

Needless to say, I was mortified. I also felt a little foolish. If what my teacher said was true, why did we go through all this trouble? I asked my parents about all this, and they tried to help me out. They also showed me the dietary guidelines God gave the Israelites in Leviticus: "And the swine, though he divide the hoof, and be clovenfooted, yet he cheweth not the cud; he is unclean to you. Of their flesh shall ye not eat, and their carcase shall ye not touch; they are unclean to you." (Leviticus 11:7-8)

My parents said that pigs do not have sweat glands. Therefore they do not get rid of the impurities as well as other animals. Many times even doctors tell their patients to get off the pork if they are having certain health problems. It takes close to 13 hours to digest pork. God made certain animals for certain functions. The pig is more of a scavenger—a living garbage can.

"But my teacher said things are different today," I told my parents. "The pigs are eating grain and corn, instead of scavenging garbage for food."

"Remember the text 'I am the Lord, I change not'?" (Malachi 3:6) my parents asked. "God's law doesn't change. God gave these principles for the health of the Israelites, and our bodies are no different today than the Israelites of old. We can be healthier, too, if we follow them today."

I tried to understand. I even learned the Bible texts and could easily show somebody from the Bible why they should not eat pork. I wanted to do right, but in my heart I still asked, "Why do we have to be so different?"

I could hardly wait until I got to high school because there, most of the games were on Tuesday and Thursday nights. At last! I could go out for sports if I wished, or at the very least, play a game of basketball with my friends.

But just when I thought my luck was going to change, my parents had a little surprise for me.

"You're not going to high school," they said. "We're sending you to a Christian boarding academy."

I was crushed. I liked living at home, had no desire to leave my friends, and could hardly wait to try out for the basketball and football teams.

"Please don't make me go!" I pleaded with my parents.

I gave them my reasons. "Fitting in" had become very important to me. Now that the games weren't on Saturday anymore, I could join the teams. Maybe be a really good player. And I didn't tell them this, but deep in my heart there was this desire to be respected. To be somebody.

When I saw that my Dad's mind was made up, I tried to persuade my mother.

"Mom, can't you see?" I pleaded. "Finally I have the chance to be somewhat normal, and you want to send me away!"

But my parents were firm. I was going to academy, and that was final.

"This is a Christian school," they told me. "It will be so much easier for you to fit in there, because they are all Christian." Their comment did interest me. Although I didn't understand all the reasons behind the rules, I did want to be a Christian.

"Wow," I thought. "A Christian school where everybody really is a Christian." I wondered what that would be like.

Regardless of my expectations, one thing was certain: wherever I went, I wanted to fit in. To be part of the crowd, and to be cool. I was tired of being "different." And so I left for academy. Not happy to be there, but with high expectations, and, unbeknownst to my parents, headed for a pile of trouble.

Gems of Thought

God's laws are for my well-being and happiness. God set me apart to protect me from the harmful results of disobedience. The dietary guidelines God gave the Israelites in Leviticus were for their health and well-being: "And the swine, though he divide the hoof, and be clovenfooted, yet he cheweth not the cud; he is unclean to you. Of their flesh shall ye not eat, and their carcase shall ye not touch; they are unclean to you" (Leviticus 11:7-8). Our bodies work the same way today as did the Isrealites.back in Bible times. God's laws haven't changed, either. "I am the Lord, I change not" (Malachi 3:6).

2

Fitting In

Academy life was a real adjustment for me, but I came to like it. Made friends, got involved in sports, and quite generally had a good time.

Actually, you might say I "majored in" having a good time. When it came to scholastics, I was never much of a student. Not that I couldn't have been. I just didn't try very hard. But I was a great "student of the crowd." At last, I could fit in! And I did.

As might be expected, there were a lot of rules in academy. I learned what good Adventists don't eat, don't listen to and don't wear. It seemed like an extremely long list of don'ts, and my view of the rules became very cynical.

"If it tastes good, it can't be good for you," I thought to myself. "If it's fun, it has to be a sin. And if the music sounds good, it has to be bad."

One of the rules I remember best had to do with hair. Guys weren't allowed to have long hair, and there were "regulations" as to just how long hair was allowed to get. Specifically, it couldn't touch your eyebrows, collar, or ears.

Many of the students hated that rule. Guys in the dorm often talked of their brothers who had graduated and grew out their hair, and we longed for that life. Mostly we just wanted freedom—freedom from the seemingly endless rules.

Once again, I was learning a set of rules while totally missing out on the reasons behind the rules. Doing most of the right things for all the wrong reasons.

Since I thought some of the rules were stupid anyway, I enjoyed getting around them whenever I could. Radios weren't allowed in the dorm rooms, but I had one. It was well hidden inside a cabinet and wired under the carpet to the door of my room. The minute the door opened, the radio went off. Just in case the dean should "bust me," I kept a few junk radios around to hand over for confiscation. I'm not proud of this now, but I thought it was pretty slick then.

Putting Vaseline on doorknobs just before the dean came around for room check was another one of my tricks. I didn't grease them all, just enough to give the dean an occasional slippery surprise. In my efforts to fool him into thinking it wasn't me, I even greased my own!

The dean wasn't stupid, of course, and made me do pushups on more than one occasion as payment for my antics. In spite of his "toughness," I really liked the dean. He was down-to-earth and took time with us. In fact, one of my secret ambitions was to be a dean someday. There were other teachers I liked, too. Some of them seemed to genuinely care.

Although I didn't get into any major trouble during my years as an underclassman, I realize now that my experiences as a freshman and sophomore set the stage for my tumultuous junior year of academy. Swearing became a part of my vocabulary early on in academy, and while I made friends, they were not a good influence.

My roommate and best friend was a guy named Daryl, and though we loved each other's company, we didn't "make good music" together. I remember my parents telling me not to hang around with Daryl. I didn't know it then, but Daryl's parents were telling him the same thing about me.

In spite of my misgivings about even attending academy, in time I came to like it there. I got really excited when I made the gymnastics team. Team members got to travel and do "shows", not to mention being looked up to as "cool" by the other students.

Fitting In

At last, I had arrived. Or so I thought.

But then came my roller coaster of a junior year. With my desire to fit in as strong as ever, I started to do some pretty "cool" things with some of my friends, like drinking and smoking pot. Although I only smoked pot once or twice during my junior year, I did do it. But something inside me said "don't go that route." Then the dean came to my room one evening and just started to talk to me. It was a meeting that I won't forget. He talked to me as if he were my friend. "Dwight," he said, "You have leadership qualities. You're a junior this year. You've been here since you were a freshman. A lot of the kids here look up to you. You could make such a difference." He was not just giving me a lecture. It was from the heart and I knew it. It made me take inventory of myself. I decided to give it a try.

I found God. I started to pray. I quit reading just about anything except the Bible, and even held student prayer groups in my room. Some nights as many as 20 or 30 kids attended. My positive change of heart had been accompanied by a similar change in grades. For the first time in my life I was actually going to make the honor roll. Unfortunately, that's when the ax fell at the root of my dreams.

"Young man, we have reason to believe you have taken drugs." I had been called into the academy principal's office, and he wanted to know if the rumors were true. They hadn't caught me, and I had only just tried it over a month before without continuing the practice.

But I was raised to be honest, and to tell the truth, even if it hurt. So I told the truth, hoping for mercy. I hoped they would have seen my turnaround, and respect me for my honesty. I hoped I might not be suspended, but given a second chance.

There was no mercy. I was kicked out, and the school was in a hurry about it, too. They wanted me out of there that very day. I saw so much hypocrisy—people saying one thing and doing another; not just the students, but the teachers also, which bugged me the most. Shouldn't they know and live it—the Christian walk—whatever that was?

So I hurried around to say goodbye to my favorite teachers, some of whom had not even heard yet that I was being kicked out. I remember that one of them cried, and I felt like crying, too.

For not wanting to go to academy, I had learned to like it there. I did not understand the mountain of rules, but I also did not want to leave. I was bitter, very bitter, about being expelled, and wondered, "What will life hold for me next?"

Gems of Thought

Following the rules, and doing the right things for the wrong reasons was boring. I wanted to fit in and be "cool," so I ignored the rules I thought were stupid, and experimented with drinking and pot. Then, when I turned my life around, and admitted my transgressions, I was punished anyway. I saw hypocrisy everywhere, and wondered where the "real" Christians were, who "walked the walk."

3

On The Bubble

I finished out that semester at the local high school, and as far as my parents were concerned, I was through with boarding academies. They felt disappointed about my experience, and, while they knew I had done wrong, they didn't like everything they had seen at the academy, either.

But I had made some really good friends in academy, and I missed them terribly. One of them was Daryl. He got into trouble before I did, so he wasn't accepted back for our junior year. By the time I was kicked out, Daryl was already attending another academy.

It's strange how the tables turn in our lives sometimes. My parents sent me to boarding academy when I didn't really want to go. Now I wanted to go back—and they didn't want to send me!

"Please let me go!" I told them. "I promise I won't get into any more trouble if you just give me another chance." Several of my friends had switched to the school Daryl was attending, and I wanted to go there, too. In the end, my parents relented, and I moved into a dorm room once more, determined to have a new start.

I had good intentions. Not wanting to disappoint my parents again, I decided to try and live a more Christian life. As part of my commitment, I went into the dormitory hall and read my Bible every night after lights had to be out in our rooms. It seemed kind of boring to me then, and I didn't understand it, but I went through the motions anyway.

I now realize that I had been really searching—searching for a geniune Christian experience. I kept looking around me—at teachers and other students—for someone who was truly living a Christian life. Someone who enjoyed their life, yet knew what it was to give 100% and surrender fully to God. Someone who might even show me the way, because the Christian life sure didn't look very appealing to me. But unfortunately, and for whatever reasons, I never did find that person during my days as an academy student.

Instead, I fell into bad company again. They weren't really bad kids, my friends. They were just "cool kids"—like Daryl—who were mostly interested in having a good time.

I didn't much care for the dean of boys at my new school either. He was much too superficial for me. You know, the kind of person who might say one thing and do another. Or talk about loving God, but strongly dislike a fellow staff member. I was really turned off by those who "talked the talk," but didn't "walk the walk."

I was also very frustrated at being kicked out of my former school. Being respected by my peers, or becoming "somebody," was very important to me. But at this point in my life I felt like a failure, a miserable failure. My parents were also very disappointed. And in my heart, I didn't want to let them down again.

Having been on the gymnastics team in the first school I attended, I was anxious to make the team in my new school as well. It didn't take long for my opportunity to come, or so I thought.

There was an opening on the team, which didn't happen very often. Because the gymnastics coach let me try out, I assumed that if I did well enough, he would let me on the team. Unfortunately, I was in for a big surprise.

"You won the tryout fair and square, Dwight," the coach told me. "But I just can't let you on the team."

"Why not?" I could hardly believe my ears.

"Well, as we both know, you were in some trouble in academy before," he answered. "You just need some time, Dwight."

Then he put his hands on my shoulders and looked me straight in the eye.

"But I will promise you one thing, Dwight," he said. "The next time we have an opening—if you win the tryout—you will have a place on the team."

Of course, coach couldn't have known at that moment that another spot would open up within a week. After all, chances to make the team didn't come up very often. I asked him about it, of course, but the coach had no intention of letting me on that soon.

"You just need more time, Dwight," was all he would say. And I was disappointed, very disappointed.

"Why did he even let me try out if he wasn't going to let me on?" I grumbled to my friends. "And why did he make things even worse by saying I won the tryout, then not letting me on?" Then there was this matter of the "next opening" that came up, which I never got to try for because it was too soon.

I felt frustrated with the system and frustrated with trying to be "good." It didn't seem like it made any difference anyway. Whether I was good or bad, I couldn't make the team. And although I was reading my Bible, I didn't know how to apply what I read in a practical way. I didn't realize it then, but something was changing inside my heart. I was tired of playing church. I wanted to be a real Christian, or none at all. But I didn't know how to go about it, and I didn't see any Christians I thought were really enjoying life.

I kept saying to myself, "Isn't the Bible true? Can't we, by God's grace, keep His commandments fully and enjoy life?"

I started to become more and more discouraged. "Lord," I said, "this Christianity is for the birds. I want this to be real. Where are your people? Does Christianity have to take a back seat? Have I come this far to see this facade? If I don't see teachers or pastors living the life of Christ, what step beyond this is there?"

So I started hanging around with Daryl again, and it didn't take us too long to get into trouble. Not for smoking pot, but for "popping" a few prescription pills brought to school by one of the guys.

I'll never forget the day I got called to the dean's office. The minute I heard the dean's voice booming my name over the dormitory loudspeaker, I knew I was in trouble. Daryl had "disappeared" from the school. Not that he ran away or anything. But he had been taken somewhere. And I was worried—genuinely worried about my best friend. In my heart, I suspected he was at the local hospital being tested for drugs—and wondered if that's what dean had in mind for me too.

"What did Daryl say to the dean?" I wondered. I knew Daryl wouldn't intentionally tell on any of his friends. But maybe he had been pressed into it.

"What does the dean know?" I wondered. It didn't take me long to find out.

"Have a seat, young man." The dean looked stern, even grim when he ushered me into his office. I took a deep breath and expected the worst.

Then came those words I wanted so badly not to hear: "Dwight, we have reason to believe that you have been taking drugs."

So! Dean must have wrung something out of Daryl. My face grew red with anger while my stomach churned into a thousand knots. I knew what I had done. Knew it was wrong. But what about the dean? He wasn't any saint himself, and I knew it. But now he was nailing me! All the frustration of the school year boiled within me, until I thought I was going to burst.

The dean's somber voice broke into my thoughts.

"I'm taking you to the hospital for a test, Dwight," he was saying, "just as soon as we get your mother's permission." He reached for the rotary phone.

"Uh, just a minute," I stuttered, my mind whirling into overdrive. I imagined the look on Mom's face when she heard the news, her disappointment, her misunderstanding of what had really happened. She would think I was on pot again! I wanted so badly to talk to her, explain to her, tell her I hadn't been smoking pot—and exactly what I had done.

"Do you think I could talk to my mother?" I begged.

"Oh no, you can't do that." The dean scowled. "You can tell your mother all about it later when we're not paying for the call. Long distance costs money, you know."

I studied his face as he dialed the number, and it didn't look kind.

"Mrs. Hall, we have reason to believe that your son's been taking drugs" the dean was curt and to the point. "We'd like your permission to have a drug test, please."

I was still thinking, fast. Dean wouldn't honor my request to speak with my mother, but what if she asked to speak with me? Suddenly all the tension and frustration and anger inside of me wanted out. Leaping to my feet, I leaned over the dean's desk and yelled loudly in the direction of the phone: "I want to talk to my mother!"

Dean gripped the receiver and swiveled around, staring at me in disbelief. As for me, I felt like a volcano in the midst of an eruption. Placing one palm on the desk, I glared and reached for the receiver, every nerve in my body shaking. He held it away and motioned for me to be still. For a moment, you could have heard a pin drop. I heard a familiar but faraway voice on the other end of the line, but I couldn't tell what she was saying. After what seemed like ages, Dean finally spoke.

"Yes, that was your son, Mrs. Hall." Another long pause. "Of course you may speak with him if you wish."

The dean glared as he handed me the phone, but I paid no attention to him. I was too busy launching into a detailed explanation of the day's events to my mother. Not one to be outmaneuvered, Dean gave me about 30 seconds to state my case.

"As I said earlier, long distance costs money," he said firmly. "And we're paying for this. You need to get off the phone."

"Will you let me call her back collect if I hang up?" I eyed the dean suspiciously. He hadn't exactly earned my trust, and I certainly didn't trust him now.

"OK, fine." Dean was brusque.

"Mom," I said, "the dean is having a fit because he said it is

23

costing him money. He said I could call you right back if I called collect."

"I will wait right here for your call," she said.

I laid down the receiver and reached to lift it again, but the dean's massive hand wrenched it away.

"Go to your room and get dressed, Hall" he growled, eyeing my casual T-shirt and shorts. "And do it NOW! You're leaving for a drug test in 10 minutes whether you like it or not."

"You said I could call her back!" I shouted, storming out of his office and toward my room.

"What is my mother thinking now?" I wondered. "She's probably worried sick, sitting by the phone and expecting me to call back any minute.

And what about Daryl? Was he OK?" My mind reeled in anger when I thought about Daryl. Why had they sent him to the hospital? Did they think he had an overdose? Were they putting him in some "rehab" program? Or sending him home? And what did they want with me, there at the hospital?

Once in my room, I threw on some old blue jeans. Then stuffing a few prize belongings into a bag, I stormed toward the door.

I didn't understand a lot of things I had seen at this Christian academy, like staff who preached one thing and lived another. Teachers who waxed eloquent when talking about brotherly love, but couldn't stand some of their fellow staff members.

After eight years in public school, I had come to a Christian school with high expectations. Unfortunately, they had not been met.

"Why am I seeing this here?" My mind charged on bitterly, not waiting for an answer. "What's with the double standards, anyway?"

I didn't know the answer to these questions, but I did know one thing: I wasn't going for any drug test. and I wasn't going home to face my parents, either. I was going to run away, and never be heard from again. And so I headed down the corridor, but not toward the dean's office. Oh no. I was headed for the fire escape. I would leave this school. I was going out on my own—to start a new life. And I wasn't ever going to come back—not for any reason, not ever.

Gems of Thought

I want to interject into this story that I truly did not see "Christians" walking the walk. That doesn't mean there weren't any. Looking back on that situation now I see that a number of these teachers were doing the best they could but who had taught them? Most of us learn to work for God but fail to walk with Him. In that time of my life I saw plenty of workers but no walkers.

4

Mom on the Line

Escaping from campus turned out to be easier than I imagined. They didn't set the fire alarm until lights out at 10:00 p.m. so I was able to walk right out the fire exit door. Then, conveniently enough, a willing village student happened to drive into the parking lot right when I needed him. Within minutes I was inside a beat-up station wagon, headed away from academy life for good.

At this point, I had two clear intentions. Number one, to call my mom as quickly as possible so that she wouldn't worry (or so I thought) and to say good-bye. Secondly, to swing by the hospital to visit Daryl—before putting this pack of bad memories behind me forever.

I asked the village student to wait a couple minutes while I made a few phone calls.

"No problem, man." My spur-of-the-minute chauffeur couldn't have been more helpful. Hurrying into the nearest phone booth, I picked up the receiver and dialed, all the while keeping a watchful eye out for the dean or other faculty members who might have come to town.

"Mom?"

"Dwight? Where are you?" Mom's voice sounded sick with worry. "I've been sitting here by the phone, waiting for you to call back."

Mom on the Line

"I tried, Mom, and he wouldn't let me." I was so angry, I nearly shouted into the phone. "I can't stand this dean, and I've had it with him and this school. These people are nothing but hypocrites."

"Where are you, Dwight?" Mom wanted to know. "Do you want me to come and pick you up?"

"No, I'm not coming home!" My voice was decisive and bitter. A wave of relief swept over me. At last—I had broken the news.

Silence reigned on the other end of the line, and I rushed to fill the gap. "It's not that I don't care about you and Dad. I just don't want to embarrass you two again. I tried to be good, Mom, really I did. But this is the second time for me. And you know, word gets around. I just can't face you and Dad."

I pushed the receiver against my ear, listening for anything, just some response from my mother. Then I realized she was crying.

"Dwight," she sobbed through her tears.

"She knows me all too well," I thought to myself. "She knows how stubborn I am, and how much I mean it."

"Dwight," my mother's voice pleaded across the miles. "Please come home."

I gripped the receiver with sweaty palms, my stomach churning again. Until now, I had mostly been thinking of my own feelings. I hadn't thought she would take it this hard.

"We all make mistakes," mom was saying. "I've made quite a few myself."

"I know, but not like this," I argued. "I've been in three schools already this year, kicked out of two."

My mind flashed back to the first academy I'd attended. How I missed being there, in spite of the rules. And how frustrated I felt at being kicked out.

"Young man, we have reason to believe you have taken drugs." Those words from the academy principal were still ringing in my ears when I heard them again—from the dean. Same song, second stanza. And now my mother was singing her own

27

little song to me too, over and over again on the phone.

"Please come home, Dwight," she pleaded. "We love you, Dwight. Whatever you do, don't go away. Promise me that you'll stay right there in the phone booth while I drive up to get you."

My mind reeled in confusion. I wanted to be on my way, but knew she was afraid to let me hang up. That if it meant talking to me all night, she would keep on, never letting me off the phone if she could help it. Tiring of the turmoil, I finally gave in.

"OK," I told her. "I promise I will not run away." Mom heaved a sigh so big I almost felt it over the phone.

"Thank you, Jesus."

Then I told her about Daryl. I was still worried about him, wondering how he was, if he was still at the hospital, and what they were doing to him.

"I'll be up to get you, Dwight," she promised, as we ended our conversation.

"Bye, mom. I love you." I hung up the receiver, drained, but determined to carry out at least part of my plan. I had to find Daryl, talk to him, and find out what had happened. If possible, I even wanted to visit him before Mom arrived. And so I reached for the phone once more. At last I would talk to Daryl—or so I thought.

Gems of Thought

Looking back on it now, I thank God for a mother who didn't give up on me. For parents who, even though they make mistakes and see their children fail, work on with love and patience for their salvation. That's what my mother did for me that night on the phone. She would not let me go!

5

De Ja Vu
With the Dean

"You've got to be kidding!"

I leaned against the door of the phone booth and scowled, not at all prepared for the voice on the other end of the line at the hospital. Was the hospital operator confused, or what? I had asked for Daryl, not the dean! Why had the operator given me the dean instead? Instinctively, I knew the answer before I ever asked the question.

The dean knew how worried I was about Daryl. He knew I would call the hospital and maybe even go there. And so Dean went to the hospital—and waited.

"Where are you, Dwight?" Dean asked me for the third time in a row.

"None of your business." It was my turn to growl. "And I didn't want to talk to you. I asked for Daryl."

"You can talk to Daryl, as soon as you've taken your drug test," the Dean persuaded.

"There's no need for any drug test," I snapped. "I'm leaving this school anyway."

"Fine, Dwight." The dean sounded confident, even jovial. "But if you want to see Daryl, you have to take the test and that's final. The hospital is cooperating with the school, and a test is what we want."

I felt confused. The drug test probably wouldn't be that bad, but on a list of events I preferred to avoid, meeting Dean again ranked lower than a root canal.

"Do you promise me I can see Daryl if I come and take the test?" The dean's motives were clearly suspect. This time, I wanted a clear understanding with the man.

"No problem, Dwight. Just come for the drug test, and then you can see Daryl." Once again, the dean had given his word. "Do you need a ride from wherever you are?"

"No, I have a ride." I hung up, knowing the village student would gladly give one more lift. Within minutes the beat-up station wagon rumbled to a stop in the hospital parking lot.

I was right about the drug test. There really was nothing to it. Unfortunately, the same thing could be said about Dean's promise to let me see Daryl while at the hospital, kind of like his promise to let me call my mother from his office and, as I later learned, his promise to Daryl not to get Daryl's friends into trouble if he told what they had done.

The test was hardly over when the dean grabbed me by the arm, growling again. "Come on," he jerked me toward the door. "I'm taking you back to the dorm, and this time you'll stay there— until your mother arrives."

I was furious, but knew from the look on Dean's face it would do no good to argue. It didn't keep me from fuming, though. And I was angry, incredibly angry at the world and the dean in particular.

In the 24 hours before my mother arrived, I had plenty of time to think. What is wrong with me? I want to do right, I have tried more than one time. Is it just the way it is? Is this my lot in life? I kept thinking, here I go again. My life seemed to change daily but not in the right direction.

All of the other guys were going to classes—going on with life as usual as if nothing had happened. They were also going to a special banquet, and I had planned to go, too. I even had a date—a nice girl who I really hoped to get to know better.

All that had changed now, of course. My date got her corsage and went to the banquet all right, but not with me. And I got a date with my mother. In the car. In spite of my wilder intentions, I was headed home. I would finish out my junior year somehow, some way at another school. And it would be my fourth school this year, wherever it was.

Gems of Thought

God has a plan, but his ways are higher than ours. Even through these difficult times God was wooing me. I was learning to walk with God without even knowing it.

6

Keeping My Word

By the time I reached home, my parents had already formulated a plan. They didn't waste any time putting it into action, either. Within a few days I was on a plane with my mother, headed for Naples, Florida. I would finish my junior year—or at least try to—in the "Sunshine State."

My dad, and uncle who owned a construction company, were already in Naples building a series of apartment complexes. In later years, my father and I would agree that his absence during both of my boarding academy crises was actually providential.

Although my dad always taught me to be honest, he did have a temper. It was the tears and sweet voice of my mother that kept me from running away for good. No one knows what would have happened if I had spoken to my father instead, but the possibility of an explosion on each end of the line was strong. Dad would have been upset and angry—just like me. In our anger, we could easily have said good-bye for good. And as my mother knew all too well, neither of us was too likely to go back on our word.

My dad was frustrated by my academy experiences, and rightfully so. My sister had a good experience at Christian schools, even loved being there. What had happened to me? My dad didn't know the answer to that question, but he had decided one thing: I wouldn't be wasting any more time in school this year. I would either salvage my grades and pass, or not go at all.

"You can just come and work for me," he said. "Get a new start in school next year." As part owner of the construction company, my dad could always find a spot for me when I needed it. So when he took me to the guidance counselor's office at Naples High School, he had just one question on his mind:

"Does Dwight have a chance to pass this year, or not?" Dad scrutinized the counselor as he leafed through my patchwork of Fs and Ds from September through April.

"Dwight has to do extremely well in everything to pass," the counselor told my dad. "As you know, Mr. Hall, there are only six weeks left in the school year."

"But if he does everything well, he can pass?" Dad was persistent.

"Well, there's always hope." The guidance counselor laughed nervously, obviously not wanting to commit himself. There wasn't much to work with here—mostly failures or near misses with a C in Art thrown in for good measure.

My dad turned to me. "Son, are you willing to put forth your best effort and do what it takes to pass?"

I knew from the look in his eyes that he wasn't fooling. That he was at the end of his rope was not hard to miss. I had better say what I meant and mean what I said. Dad was a man of his word, and expected the same from me.

"I can do it, Dad." My resolution was hardly out when the counselor broke in.

"But Mr. Hall," the counselor protested. "He'll have to do everything right. And his past record just doesn't . . ."

"Did you hear my son?" Dad thundered back. "He said he'd do it. He can. And he will." Case closed.

"Yes, Mr. Hall," the counselor answered meekly, though he never did wipe that wait-and-see look off his face.

As for me, I walked out of the counselor's office with my head held high, feeling like a man. To hear my Dad tell the counselor "Did you hear my son? He said he'd do it." And then for him to say "He can and he will," made me feel so good. After all the mistakes

I had made Dad still put his confidence in me. I would hit the books and show myself trustworthy. I might not be perfect—after all, I had learned a few bad habits during the past few months. But this would be a new start of sorts. I would do what I could to keep my word, and hope that the guidance counselor would keep his.

Gems of Thought

As I look back on it now, I see that Dad's absence during those critical times of my life was much more than coincidence. It wasn't like Dad went to Naples for an extended stay very often. In fact, he only went twice during my high school career. As incredible as it may seem, both of those times "just happened" to be the same times I was kicked out of boarding academy. God's timing is always perfect.

7

Buckling Down

The next six weeks were a grueling experience. School, study, sleep, school, study, and sleep—day in and day out. Actually, that part of it wasn't too different from academy life.

In academy, my workday in the dough factory started at 4 a.m. five days a week. I had to get up by 3:30 to make it to work on time, so I never got enough sleep. I got out of work at 8 every morning, a full 13 minutes before the start of my first class.

Of course I wanted breakfast, so there was this mad dash to the cafeteria every morning during my 13-minute interlude, during which I stuffed a few morsels into my mouth. Then off to Biology II and the perennial struggle to stay awake. Thanks to classes, sports, study hall, and a host of other activities, I had a hard time getting to bed by 10:00 p.m. when they turned out the lights. I often only had a measly 3-4 hours of sleep.

Looking back on that whirlwind of a schedule, its no wonder that my attitude, my grades, and my spiritual experience suffered. My grueling schedule left hardly any time for reflection or relaxation, not to mention some much-needed rest. And that, together with my drug-related problems at both academies, contributed to my sense of failure. I was learning perfectly to be busy, so busy, I had no time to be still and know God (Psalms 46:10).

I added to the problem by taking an especially heavy schedule of classes. By taking extra courses, I hoped to graduate after my junior year. That didn't work out, but the extra credits did come in handy right when I needed them in Florida.

Things went better for me at Naples High School. All my hard work those last six weeks did pay off. In spite of the repeated school switching and tempestuous turn of events that had plagued my junior year, I managed to salvage a passing grade and move on. At last—a reigning senior!

That summer and the following school year found me working as planned for my dad's and uncle's construction company. It was hard physical labor, but I didn't mind. I had a sporty muscle car—a sleek black Cobra—to show for my efforts, and the freedom to have a good time.

During the second semester of my senior year, I didn't even have to go to class. With enough credits to graduate, I enrolled in an OJT (on the job training) program and worked for my dad until June. Then I stopped in at the school, got measured for my cap and gown, and marched with the rest of my class.

Although I had "buckled down" scholastically, at least enough to earn passing grades in public school, nothing else about me had really changed. For my parents, I tried to be the same Dwight they had always known. As far as possible, I gave the appearance of "flying straight." Nights out with my friends were a different story, however. I may have learned to smoke, drink and cuss in a Christian school—but I found it easy to continue those habits while in public school.

It was while in Florida that I really developed a taste for beer, and, once again, it was with my good friend Daryl. Daryl had run away from home, then moved in with us for a while. This was bad news for me spiritually, but I don't think my parents realized the danger I was in. I still wanted to do God's will, but I kept making the wrong decisions.

One hot Florida day when Daryl and I were out cruising around, he stopped to pick up a six-pack of beer.

"Man, this is really good stuff," Daryl said. "You should try some, Dwight. I know you'll like it."

Buckling Down

Wanting to be cool, I popped the top off a can and took a swig. The taste was horrible, and it was all I could do to gulp it down.

"Not bad, huh?" Daryl wanted to know. I nodded and tried to agree. When he was looking my way, I faked taking another swig. But I was much more interested in draining the rest of my can out the window—a task which I managed bit by bit, in between mouthfuls of chips whenever Daryl looked the other way.

It still amazes me how hard we will work to acquire a taste for something that's bad for us. We do all we can to fit in with people—even if they don't "fit" in with us. We aren't willing to work at acquiring a taste for spinach or broccoli, yet so many people will work at acquiring a taste for something like beer or even coffee. That's the way it was with me.

Several days after my first failed drink of beer, I decided to try again. I didn't really plan it that way—it just happened. This time the day was incredibly hot and I was really sweating it out. Stopping by a convenience store for gas, I decided to pick up a pop as well. But when I reached into the cooler, there was a beer sitting there right in front of my face, as if to say "drink me, drink me!" And for some unexplainable reason, it tempted me. So I bought it, drinking it right down. It turned out to be so refreshingly cold that it didn't taste all that bad. Little by little, I developed a taste for beer until I really did love it. I wish I had put the same type of effort into acquiring a love for the right as I did for the wrong.

Although Mom and Dad didn't have solid evidence of my bad habits, they had their suspicions. Being a nurse, Mom knew exactly what to look for. I didn't make it easy. To cover up the telltale smells, I kept chewing gum and a bottle of cologne in the glove box of my Cobra. The minute I walked into the house every night, I downed a glass of milk (another cover-up tactic), then headed straight for my room, although I had to walk through the living room and say hello to get there. So many times as I went through this nightly routine, I felt the eyes of my mother upon me. She never said anything then, but later I learned that she had indeed suspected me.

"Darwin," she said to my father one night, "I believe Dwight is on something."

"Better leave him alone," my dad replied. "If he comes in staggering around or falling on the floor, I will kick him out." Dad sighed. He knew as well as Mom did that if they confronted me, I would leave. And in spite of his misgivings, he felt it was better to let me be, unless I was doing something obvious.

During that time and even in later years, I kept going to church. Although I was far from God, church attendance still seemed important to me for some unknown reason. I knew it wouldn't save me, but I felt so strong about going to church. It kept me in touch. I felt that if I cut off all ties, it would be the end of my faith—at least whatever faith you call it. Somehow I felt it kept me in touch. Also, I was afraid that if I quit I would never come back again. So even if I closed the bars at 2:30 a.m. I still showed up when church started at 9:30—sick stomach and all. And I always wondered, in fact it really bothered me, why people who were "better Christians" than I was (e.g. they didn't cuss or drink) couldn't make it to Sabbath School on time.

"If, as you say, Jesus is so important to you," I wanted to ask them, "why can't you make it to Sabbath School? If Christ is first in your life, shouldn't Sabbath be the most important day of the week to you? And what message does this give your children?" I guess I was really turned off by the low or even lacking Sabbath School habits among our members. After all, I was always there on time—even if I did have a major hangover.

When the gas "shortage" hit in 1974, Dad moved back to Michigan. The apartment complexes were finished, and with them his employment in Florida.

Since I was working for my dad, my job was supposed to end with his. However, I had made a few good friends in Florida and didn't want to leave. One of my friends was a guy named Roy. Like me, Roy drove a souped-up muscle car. We often worked on our cars together, and had a great time. Roy didn't smoke pot, so when I was around him, I didn't either. And it was no big deal.

Buckling Down

Toward the end of my senior year, I had met and really fallen for a girl. She was sweet, pretty, and fun—the only things that mattered to me at that point in time. In fact, our relationship had progressed to the point that we were even talking about marriage.

Of course, she was no Christian, nor did she pretend to be. Although I didn't really think her religious beliefs mattered to me then, ideas from my past kept bothering me. I could see that many of the ideas I had been brought up with weren't important to her. Also, I believed it wasn't wise for a believer to be "unequally yoked" with an unbeliever. As I look back on it now, it seems strange that these things even mattered to me at that point. After all, I wasn't exactly living an exemplary life myself.

In spite of these potential drawbacks, I knew I loved her and really wanted to marry her. I didn't want to leave Roy, either. But, everything changed for me when my father moved back to Michigan. Most importantly, I lost my job. Normally, this wouldn't have been a problem for me, but the economy was worse than bad at that time.

I was willing to do anything—even pump gas—if only I could stay in Naples. But in spite of my near-Herculean efforts, I failed to find a job. With my wallet nearly empty and my gas tank approaching the same state, I came to grips with reality. There might be no job for me in Florida, but there was one waiting for me in Michigan, with my dad.

And so I said goodbye to my newfound friends. Florida, a high school diploma, and all the unhappy experiences of my junior year were all behind me now. I was going up north again—for another "new start."

Gems of Thought

"Busy-ness" is one of Satan's greatest weapons. We will never walk with God when we have no time. And even when I was deeply entrenched in a life of sin, I always made it to church. That is one reason I advise each of you to never, and I mean never, give

39

up! You are only a failure when you quit.

The Bible text that comes to my mind is in 2 Timothy 3:5, "Having a form of godliness, but denying the power thereof. . . ." If our children and youth are to be in the heavenly kingdom, Moms and Dads, we need to quit playing church. Our children can see right through us. They are just more honest than we are. My reason for sharing these experiences in this book are so you might see that these problems exist in many of us. We all are usually good at something. I happened to make it to Sabbath School but had other deep seated problems. The bottom line is we don't have an experiential love for God. It might be the preacher that has such superficial and suffocating sermons, but why does that affect us? Are we looking to man instead of to the author and finisher of our faith? Let us take the time to meditate on this, and ask God to help us overcome our shortcomings, even being late to church.

8

Escape to Adventure

L ife in Michigan found me reunited with Daryl once again. We shared an apartment and I worked for my Dad. At last—I was on my own.

But while I was a construction worker by day, I was still a definite "partier" by night. Away from the watchful eyes of my mother and with no deans to confront me, I could do pretty much as I pleased. And I did.

During the 12-hour days spent on construction jobs, I was hardworking and responsible. So much in fact, that my dad wanted to make me a foreman. That presented a problem because I didn't really want to work any harder. In fact, longer hours and more responsibility didn't appeal to me at all. I was much more interested in cruising Coldwater in my sleek black Cobra, checking out the girls.

Although I was mostly interested in having a good time, I also wanted to travel and to learn to fly. Most of all, I wanted to be some-body. My self-image had never quite recovered from the beating it took my junior year, and I really had something to prove. While I hadn't the foggiest idea of what I wanted to do with my life, I did know I wanted to amount to something, to be respected and, most of all, to be successful.

When I was young, I was always taught that a Christ-like life was the only way to real happiness and success. But I hadn't ever seen it the way the Bible explained it. So I thought I would go the way of the world.

I never intended to join the service. In fact, I thought people who did were pretty stupid. But one day I walked by a recruiting station in downtown Coldwater, and for some reason, decided to check it out.

The recruiter on duty that day was no dummy. He asked me what I wanted to do in life. So I told him. I wanted to learn to fly, to travel, to avoid college, to make good money and to have an even better time. I even told him I wanted to be somebody.

"You can do all of that, and more, in the army," the recruiter said.

My eyes widened. He had my full attention then, and he knew it.

"Listen," he started. "I can get you a job you will really enjoy. You want to take it easy, travel, and have a good time, right? How about driving an army truck in Hawaii?"

Now, driving truck in Hawaii sounded a whole lot more interesting than pounding nails in Coldwater. In my mind's eye, I saw myself in the islands—deeply tanned, surfing, soaking up the sun on a beach surrounded by beautiful scenery and even more beautiful girls, which is why within minutes, I did the unthinkable and signed up for what I thought would be a life of fun in the sun.

My parents were deeply disappointed. Among other things, they feared for my spiritual welfare in the service. I wasn't living a Christian life as it was, and in the army, they thought things could get even worse. They just didn't understand why I hadn't discussed this issue with them. They explained the principles to me that one mind is not sufficient to make big decisions. Even God that created us gave us this counsel in His Word.

How important those words of wisdom were.

"Iron sharpeneth iron; so a man sharpeneth the countenance of his friend" (Proverbs 27:17). "In the multitude of counselors there is safety" (Prov. 11:14; 13:10; 15:22).

My parents' apprehension didn't dim my enthusiasm in the

slightest, however. I was even more elated after passing the required physical in Detroit and talking to the recruiting officer there.

"Dwight," he said, "you passed the physical with flying colors."

This was music to my ears, especially after the accumulation of failures still fresh in my mind from high school.

"In fact," the recruiter went on, "you did so well that we want you to consider going into a special unit." He paused meaningfully before delivering the punch line: "We have just a few openings for a few select men."

"Really?" I sat up straight in my chair and looked the recruiter eye to eye.

"These are tough units," he went on. "The one I'd like to put you in is the Airborne Rangers, which is kind of like the Green Berets. You say you'd like to fly?"

"Yes sir!" I could hardly stay in my chair.

"Well, the Airborne Rangers get to jump out of airplanes," he went on. "They wear a black beret, and because of their bravery they are the first ones to go into battle."

The recruiter pulled out a picture of a solidly muscled Ranger and leaned forward earnestly, eyeing my slender frame.

"Do you see this picture, Dwight?"

"Yes sir."

"Well, when the Airborne Rangers get done with you, your body will look like this. We're in the business of turning men just like you into lean, mean fighting machines."

That promise really struck an answering chord in my self-conscious soul. Back in academy, the girls used to comment about how skinny I was.

"You have a really cute smile, Dwight," was one of their favorite lines, "but unfortunately, when you turn sideways you disappear."

The decision to be an Airborne Ranger instead of a truck driver in Hawaii was a no brainer for me. Sure, I wanted to have fun in the sun and travel. But I could do that as a Ranger too. Best of all, as an Airborne Ranger I would finally be somebody.

I could hardly wait to tell my parents and friends all about it as soon as I got home.

"I'm going to be an Airborne Ranger," I told them. "Part of an elite unit in the army, where they only have room for a few good men."

My Cobra couldn't run the Coldwater streets fast enough as I sped down to the recruiting office in Coldwater, anxious to tell the officer of my good fortune.

"You have got to be crazy," he gasped, shaking his head. "When the Airborne Rangers go into battle, they have the shortest life expectancy of anybody."

While I was surprised at his response, the recruiting officer's cautionary words didn't faze me one bit. In fact, the idea of defying death excited me all the more. I would get to fly. I would get to travel. There would be fun and adventure. And most importantly of all—at last, I would be somebody.

Gems of Thought

As a general rule, one mind is not sufficient to make big decisions. Even God that created us gave us this counsel in His Word. How important those words of wisdom were. We should always get another person's opinion. Just make sure it is from somebody you know who has wisdom in that area. So often when we do get feedback, we go to people that will agree with us. Be wise and don't pick out someone who will just agree with you. I guarantee you, you will save a lot of heartache. "Iron sharpeneth iron; so a man sharpeneth the countenance of his friend" (Proverbs 27:17). "In the multitude of counselors there is safety" (Proverbs 11:14; 13:10; 15:22).

9

The Perfect Soldier

Life in the Airborne Rangers was tougher than tough, but I rose to the challenge. Our superiors focused on one goal— preparing their charges for battle—and they did a pretty good job of it.

Physically, there were constant marches, maneuvers and workouts. Like jumping off of a 3-foot wall over and over again. We had to land just right, and then get up in the next breath. If we didn't, a sergeant yelled in our ears and kicked sawdust in our faces.

The Airborne Rangers worked on your mind, too. We had to focus every inch of our being on an enemy, hate that enemy, and want to kill that enemy. In the 1970s the "enemy of choice" was the communists. I remember sitting in the army bleachers with 50 or more guys, and the sergeant yelling, "Who wants to kill a commie today?" And we would all shout, "I do! I do! I do!" And we did that over and over again.

Basic training was so tough that when it was over, only 7 soldiers out of more than a hundred got their private stripes (or "mosquito wings," as we called them). I was proud to be in that number.

The next "step up" was Advanced Individualized Training, or AIT. In some ways, AIT made basic training look easy, but once again I rose to the challenge. I wanted to turn my body into that "lean mean fighting machine," to be successful in something I did—to be somebody. When AIT was over, once more I stood proudly among the few first time "achievers."

I wish I could say all this made me happy, but I can't. There was a nagging emptiness in my heart, a void I tried in vain to fill by being a model soldier.

While I was in the Airborne Rangers I continued to attend church when I could. In my own way, I even tried to keep the Sabbath. If my unit marched over to the camp store, I went along but wouldn't buy anything because it was Sabbath.

Clinging to some of my childhood convictions didn't keep me from drinking, however. It seemed as though everyone in the service drank and drank heavily. There wasn't much else to do in the evenings, and since being a model soldier hadn't taken away the void in my life, I tried to fill it with drink. While I never got heavily into hard liquor or drugs, I drank beer by the cartons. In addition, I frequented some places that I am now ashamed to mention.

Night after night I staggered back to the barracks, drunk. But somehow, maybe from force of habit, I knelt by my bed to pray. But because I knew that God would hear a sincere prayer, I also knew He would be the only one who could take care of my burden, the burden of guilt. He alone I could trust. I wanted to surrender to Him, but I didn't know how. Other people said they had surrendered, but their actions did not show the precious victory I longed to experience. So, there by my bunk, I would bury my face in the green wool army blanket and talk to God.

In my heart I knew that something was drastically wrong. That I wasn't happy, and something very important was missing from my life. My prayers went something like this: "Lord, I know I am going to hell," I would say. And I was sure of it, for the Bible itself said that "the wages of sin is death." I knew I was living a life of sin, but I also didn't want to be a hypocrite. I figured if I was going to hell, at least I would go honestly. I told God all of this, and also about my determination not to play church or be a pretender.

The Perfect Soldier

Sometimes after a night out on the town, when I was driving around in my little yellow truck, I would go find myself a quiet road and drive down it. Then I would stop by a field, and just sit there thinking—and look up at the stars.

"Is there really a God up there?" I would wonder to myself. "If there is, I hope He will help me straighten out my life." And although I wasn't acting on it, in my heart I had this desire to be a "real" Christian, whatever that was. I did know for sure that a real Christian, and I mean real, would do what is right to be happy.

About this time I started getting pretty frustrated with the Airborne Rangers. Earning my mosquito wings and becoming a PFC (one step higher than a private) so early in the game had taken away much of the challenge for me.

According to Army rules, I couldn't be promoted to sergeant until after at least three years in the service. In the meantime, I was stuck with subordination to a group of other sergeants in the barracks. And when I say subordination, I do mean subordination. These guys took great pleasure in ordering the privates around. Whenever I passed them in the hall, which was really quite frequently, they would make me stand at attention. And, in contrast to my feelings, they enjoyed every minute of it.

Then I started to think about what I had "accomplished" in the Airborne Rangers. True, I had been a model soldier. But I didn't get to do the things that were promised me when I enlisted. Other than jumping out of a few airplanes, I didn't get to fly. Except for being stationed in Seattle (which was a nice city but not exactly Hawaii), I didn't get to travel, either. And I spent a lot more time in the bars than I ever did on the beach.

I was unhappy, dissatisfied with my life. This hypocritical life was everywhere. A promise was one thing but following through was something else. I just wanted real live honest people. I might have accomplished my goal to be "somebody," but I sure didn't have the peace I wanted. So one night on my knees, after I had been in the Airborne Rangers for about a year, I started talking to

God about it. I was pretty drunk that night, but I asked God for three things anyway:

1. To get me out of the service early
2. To help me find a girl that would not like to party—that would love children, want to stay home and take care of them, and love being a wife to me, and
3. To help me get to know Him—intimately know Him. I wanted a real experience with God.

"Lord, if you are out there, and if you are real, please show me," I prayed. "I want to walk with you."

"I've heard all about people like Elijah, Moses, John the Baptist, and Enoch in the Bible, Lord," I prayed. "But where are those people today? The people who put you first in everything—and I mean everything?"

In my heart, I desperately wanted to be a Christian. At the same time, I was determined not to be a hypocrite. And I certainly didn't want to be a fake.

So many times I remember telling the Lord how unhappy I was, that I didn't want to live to just exist. As I looked around me I saw people at every stage of life. Most were just going through the motions. When I looked at the older people who wouldn't be on planet earth much longer, they seemed to have no hope of a better life.

"There's got to be more than this, God," I prayed. "Please help me."

Little did I realize that God would answer all three of my requests—although not all at the same time.

My first answer to prayer came when I received an early release from the service. Getting out of the Airborne Rangers into another branch of the service wasn't hard, because the Rangers were a voluntary unit. All I had to do was tell my superior that I wanted to be out. Still, it was a struggle for me. In spite of my resolve, it seemed I was throwing all my hard-earned accomplishments down the drain. In addition, quitting the Army early seemed like another failure to me. I wanted to finish what I had started.

The Perfect Soldier

In spite of these misgivings, I stuck to my decision and was soon transferred to a different unit. Once in my new unit, I managed to befriend the captain, and he really did seem to respect me. Part of it was that I was a "gung ho" soldier. I was also very neat. All my uniforms were tailored exactly for my size. My shirts were starched, shoes spit-shined, and fatigues tapered to fit just right.

I can still remember the day I told the Captain I wanted to quit. Not wanting to leave anything to chance, I thought through my speech carefully in advance. I thought about what I would say, and what the captain might say, and how I would respond.

When I finally got up my nerve, I marched into his office dressed in my finest uniform and stood at attention, as was the army custom.

"Parade rest," The captain commanded. Then, "What's on your mind, Hall?"

"Sir, I want out of this man's army sir," I replied.

He was shocked at my request, and he didn't attempt to hide it. After all, I had been an all-out, highly committed soldier. At first, he didn't think I was really serious.

"Oh, that's great, Hall," he said sarcastically. "I want out of this man's army. Do you just think I will let you out?"

Fortunately, I had anticipated this reaction from him, and even planned what I would say next.

"May I have permission to speak, sir?" I asked.

"Permission granted."

Then I explained my situation. That no matter how hard I worked, there was nothing left to achieve for another year and a half; that a year and a half seemed like a very long time to me; that this routine and being bossed around by all the sergeants seemed like worthless living to me. That life was too important for me to just "bum around" in the army for another year.

"Well, what if we send you to school?" He inquired. "If you sign up for another four years, I'll send you to officer's training school."

I wasn't the least bit interested in that option.

"Sir, I don't want to sign up for another four years," I replied. "I just want out, now."

"What will you do?" The captain peppered me with questions. "Are you sure you can find a job?"

"I'm not worried about finding a job," I told him. "I know I can always work for my dad in construction."

In the end, the captain offered to call my dad and talk with him about the situation. This was unheard of in the army, but he did it. Then he gave me a little advice.

"There's no reason for me to let you out of here, Hall," he said, "although I suppose if you were to be a bad influence on the other soldiers I would have to let you go." Then he said he could get me out, but it would have to be a general discharge under honorable conditions.

This was music to my ears. After all my hard work, I couldn't bear the thought of a dishonorable discharge. It was even hard on me to give up my starch and creased uniforms, but I decided to do it anyway. I wanted to make sure the captain had reason to let me out of the army.

In the end, that didn't bother me. I was just so happy to be getting out—and a whole year early. During my days in the service I kept in close contact with my parents. Now, my mom flew out to Seattle to meet me. Together we loaded my few belongings into the yellow "Chevy Luv" truck I had bought out west, and headed for Michigan.

During this entire situation, I was very much aware that God had answered my prayer. He helped me out of the service.

And now, once again, I was going for a ride with my mother. Only this time, I wanted to. And in the back of my mind, I was starting to wonder. If God helped me get out early, would He do something more for my life? What about the "finding a wife" part of my prayer?

The Perfect Soldier

Gems of Thought

Although I was living a life of sin, I knew that God would hear a sincere prayer. But, little did I realize then that God would answer all three of my most heartfelt requests, in ways I could not have foreseen. He answered my first prayer right away, getting me out of the military early, with an honorable discharge!

10

"Dwight, This is Deb"

T he answer to my second prayer started to materialize a few months after I got out of the service. Once again I was working for my dad, and the girl I was dating was a waitress at the local Big Boy restaurant.

One evening my girlfriend and I were just sitting down to dinner when an acquaintance of hers walked in with her date.

"Deb, come over here," my date motioned and jumped out of her seat. "I want you to meet Dwight."

Then to me she said, "Dwight, I want you to meet a good friend of mine."

Something about Deb caught my attention immediately. Not just that she was beautiful, which she was, but there was something about her. And my heart was already saying, "I want to know this girl better."

Dwight didn't know it at the time, but I wanted to get better acquainted, too. Not that I was boy-crazy or anything like that. I was only 16 at the time. But Dwight's girlfriend was a close friend of mine, and had told me all about this "cute guy who just got out of the service." So she kind of piqued my interest.

The night I met Dwight, my date and I were cruising around town. Dwight was out cruising too, and every time he passed, he would honk and wave.

"Do you know that guy?" My date wanted to know after Dwight had met up with and waved at us about three times.

"Not really, but I want to," I almost replied. But instead I just said "No."

"Then stop waving at him," said my date. So the next time Dwight drove by and waved, I acted like I didn't see him. But of course, I didn't feel very good about it.

Fortunately for me, I "ran into" Deb again the very next night. I was out with the guys and headed to the bar when we stopped by McDonalds to pick up some pop. We were actually on our way out the door when I noticed Deb on her way in.

While Deb was making her way into a line at McDonalds, I was thinking fast. Wanting to buy some time and go back to talk with her, I "accidentally" dropped my comb. As I reached to pick it up, our eyes met and that was all the encouragement I needed! I told the guys to wait a minute and went back in to talk with her. After making small talk for a few minutes, I got straight to the point.

"Would you like to go for a ride with me?" I asked. Although the guys were waiting for me outside, and even motioning for me to hurry up, I was eager to make other plans.

When Dwight first asked me to take a ride with him, I said no. Even though I wanted to get to know him, my better judgment told me to be careful. After all, he was an older guy and I was barely 16. My courage rose, however, when I saw my brother drive into the parking lot. Randy was 2 years older than me, and wiser. After asking Dwight to wait a minute, I ran over to talk to Randy.

"Randy," I said, "I want to go for a ride with that guy over there. Could you do me a favor?"

Believe me, this is not what I recommend for young

girls to do. But I asked my brother to stay in the parking lot, right by his car, and watch for me to ride by occasionally. He promised that he would. More than that, Randy said if I didn't come around every so often, he would come find me—wherever I was.

Gems of Thought

Deb was the answer to my second prayer. I praise Him now for giving her to me at that point in my life.

11

A Growing Relationship

Deb and I really hit it off during our ride that night. So I asked her for a date that weekend. At first she said yes, but when I ran into her at McDonalds again that week, Deb told me she had just gotten a new job and couldn't go out because she had to work. I thought she was just brushing me off, so I decided I probably wouldn't ask her out again.

I really did have to work that night, but then my schedule got changed. However, I didn't call Dwight to tell him about the schedule change—at least not at first. Why I called him the next Saturday evening I'll never know, because I just didn't call guys. But I did, and told him what had happened.

"Well, do you want to go out tonight?" I asked Deb when she called. She said yes, so I asked her if she could be ready in an hour.

"Yes," she said again. I didn't know it then, but she was ready to go right away. From that night on, I started seeing Deb almost every single day. And right from the start, I felt sure she was the one for me. In fact, about three months into our relationship I was so sure that I told her so.

"Deb, we're going to get married," I said.

But Deb wasn't so sure. "Oh, you think so, Dwight?" was all

she would say. "No, I don't think so," I insisted. "I know we're going to get married." Having dated a number of girls in my life, I knew in my heart that Deb was the one for me. I also felt, somehow, that getting married would settle me down. After we got married, I reasoned, we would have a nice home, then children, and even attend church regularly like my parents did.

Well, I really liked Dwight. But when he first told me he thought we would get married, I had only known him 3 months! Besides that, I was sixteen years old and a junior in high school. Dwight was so sure of it all. And he kept saying, "We're going to get married, Deb." After hearing this for about five months, I started to believe it!

Then Dwight started talking about getting married that next summer. I didn't say anything to my parents for a while, but one day I decided it was time. Not having the nerve to be too direct about it, I asked my mother a question.

"Mom," I asked, "if I marry Dwight, what relation would he be to you?" I knew the answer, of course, but just wanted to hear my mother's reaction.

"He'd be my son-in-law," she replied without a moment's hesitation.

"Well, what would you think of that?" I asked.

My mother looked thoughtful for a moment.

"I like Dwight," she answered. End of conversation.

Although Deb and I got along very well, there were a few bumps in our relationship. One time we were at a party and I was drinking with the guys. Deb had a few drinks too, and I didn't like what I saw. Although I drank quite a bit myself, I was pretty responsible in a lot of other ways. I always went to work on time, worked a lot of hours, never called in sick, and even attended church on a regular basis. And in my heart, I had made up my mind to marry a girl who was not a "partier."

Deb could tell I was upset, so we just left. After we got in my truck, a guy came up to me and asked for a light. I didn't have one, but when I told him so, he called me a name. Now, I wasn't the type to act like I was bigger than somebody else, but I also didn't like being pushed in a corner. And this guy made me so mad, my instincts from the Airborne Rangers started to kick in. So I decided to grab him around the neck and speed up to about 30 miles an hour in my 4-wheel drive. You know, give him a nice little "ride" and then drop him off. Fortunately, calmer heads prevailed. Although Deb put a quick halt to the idea, she couldn't stop my anger—and I drove her home at very high speeds.

When Dwight took me home that night, I knew something was wrong. But even though I knew something was wrong at the party, I thought the major part of Dwight's frustration was that bigmouthed guy in the parking lot. So I was shocked when he told me what was really wrong.

"Deb," he said, "I just don't know if this is going to work."

"Well, why not?" I wanted to know, feeling really hurt.

"Well, I really want to marry a girl who is not a partier, and who doesn't drink."

I was really surprised at this, because Dwight drank quite freely himself. But drinking was never a big deal with me. In fact, I didn't care for the taste of beer at all.

"Well, then, I'm just the girl you're looking for," I told him. "I don't like to drink, and I don't like to party."

"You mean you don't like to drink?" Dwight couldn't believe it.

"No," I told him. "I really don't like the taste of beer. And besides that, Dwight, if it would make you happy for me not to drink, I'll stop drinking." And I did.

As I look back on our relationship I see that my

love for Dwight was strong. I was willing to do anything within reason for him. My only thoughts were that I just wanted to make him happy. If he was happy I knew I would be.

Gems of Thought

If my partner is happy I know I will be. That's how our walk with God should be and will be if we truly have a relationship with him. As David says in the Bible in Psalms 40:8," I delight to do thy will."

12

Deb Studies the Bible

Unfortunately, my lifestyle hadn't changed much since my days with the Airborne Rangers. Although I had been raised in a Christian home, I was still a partier, still a drinker, still mostly interested in having a good time.

In contrast to my wild way of life, Deb was a quiet girl who didn't party or drink. Not that she had grown up going to church on a weekly basis, because she hadn't.

Meeting me changed all of that for her. In spite of my wayward lifestyle, I had high aspirations for my future home, and it wasn't long before I began taking Deb to church. On weekends when I took Deb to church, she genuinely seemed to enjoy it.

Although I did enjoy church, I have to admit that not all of my motives for attending were religious. I felt that if Dwight and I were to marry, we should share a common faith. I was also very much aware that if I wanted to marry Dwight in that church, I would have to be baptized.

Although there were some major gaps between my own lifestyle and personal belief system, I enjoyed showing Deb the Bible verses relating to lifestyle. In spite of my poor example, it's amazing how open she was to it all. Every time I told her something new,

59

she just said, "Show it to me in the Bible." So I showed her what the Bible had to say about eating pork, and keeping the Sabbath, and a number of other lifestyle issues.

One night we went out to eat, and Deb got a ham sandwich. And it really bothered me.

"Deb," I said, "the Bible says you shouldn't eat ham."

"Show me in the Bible," Deb replied. Turning to Leviticus 11:7, I read where God told His people not to eat unclean meats.

"Our stomachs are no different than the Israelites' were way back then," I told her. "So if God said it wasn't best to eat pork then, it's not good today either." I also shared some other health information I knew, about how pork raises the cholesterol level and takes 13 hours to digest in the stomach. And so Deb stopped eating ham. Another time I said something to her about jewelry.

"Show me that in the Bible," Deb said again.

So I read to her from 1Timothy 2:9-10, where it talks about women adorning themselves with modest apparel, not with "gold or pearls or costly array", but with good works.

This was no problem for Deb, because she didn't wear much jewelry or makeup anyway. Her usual outfit included one ring and a couple of small earrings. And as I look back on it now, that was one of the things that attracted me to her. She was so natural, so beautiful just the way she was, and I told her so. She stopped wearing her jewelry, even though I never told her to.

For the Sabbath, I showed Deb the fourth commandment:

"Remember the sabbath day, to keep it holy. Six days shalt thou labour and do all thy work: But the seventh day is the sabbath of the Lord thy God: in it thou shalt not do any work, thou, nor thy son, nor thy daughter, thy manservant, nor thy maidservant, nor thy cattle, nor thy stranger that is within thy gates: For in six days the Lord made heaven and earth, the sea, and all that in them is, and rested the seventh day: wherefore the Lord blessed the sabbath day, and hallowed it" (Exodus 20:8-11).

"But I thought that commandment was nailed to the cross," Deb countered.

Deb Studies the Bible

"It just doesn't make sense that one commandment would be done away with, while the others remain," I replied. "It's not OK to lie, steal, commit adultery or kill, so why would it be OK to break God's holy Sabbath day?"

"If the seventh day is the Sabbath, why do so many people go to church on Sunday then?" Deb wanted to know.

"Many people don't know what the Bible says," I told her. Many don't even take their Bibles to church anymore—much less read them. So whatever the pastor says, they do. And if they were raised going to church on Sunday, they just go without even thinking about it. Even the church I go to the same holds true.

"It's not the day that saves you," I told her. But if God said we should keep the seventh day, then we should keep it."

Deb had no problem with my answers, so she started keeping the Sabbath. But I never did show her the texts about drinking. "Wine is a mocker, strong drink is raging: and whoseover is deceived thereby is not wise" (Proverbs 20:1).

I knew about those texts, of course. I knew drinking was wrong, and that I could not be saved in that condition. But I also didn't want to be a hypocrite. I didn't want to quit drinking, and then miss it everyday of my life. I wanted to quit drinking for the right reasons, and it just wasn't a commitment I was willing to make at that point in my life. But I knew I would have to deal with it someday, and work it out by myself.

Little did I know then that the God of heaven was wooing me little by little. Even though we are in a lost condition, His love is unconditional. I praise Him now for giving me Deb at that point in my life. Somehow, I had to convince her parents to let me marry her. But how would I do this?

Gems of Thought
Little did I know then that the God of heaven was wooing me little by little. Even though we are in a lost condition, His love is unconditional.

13

Engaged at Last!

I'll never forget the afternoon Dwight and I talked with my parents about marriage. We all sat around the kitchen table, while my mother asked Dwight question after question.

One of the big questions was whether or not I would finish high school. That was very important to my parents, and it was important to me too. Dwight promised that I would finish, and I was so proud of him. He seemed to have an answer for every question my mother asked.

My father was a different story. Dwight knew him well by this time, since they shared a beer and an hour or two of conversation nearly every night after Dwight took me home. But this time, he didn't say a thing. In fact, all I could hear was his breathing.

Finally, he got weary of the whole conversation and slammed his fist on the table so loudly it made me jump.

"If you two want a wedding," he thundered, "you'd better get busy and do it. Because I'm not going to take any time off from farming."

It was his own way of saying that we had his permission to get married. As I turned to look at him, I could see him smile.

Engaged at Last!

Deb planned to be baptized before our marriage so we would also be united in our faith. Our pastor, however, refused to baptize her as long as she wore an engagement ring. We were especially bothered that the pastor's wife wore a rather large brooch, and wore it quite often. This upset both of us, to the point that we wouldn't even stay for church whenever he preached.

Deep down, I understood the rules, but how could Christians I kept wondering, if they knew their Bible, be so inconsistent? I knew I wasn't a Christian, and I knew why. I didn't try to hide it. I longed to see a happy, consistent Christian who would actually walk the walk. Lord, I kept saying. Where are they? I know you have to have laws. They protect us and put a hedge around us, but do we have to play hide-and-go-seek to find them? If that's the case, I give up. I will be glad to let you win. Just show me some real, true Christians.

Like most couples, we had a few things to work out even during our engagement. On one particular occasion, I wanted Dwight to help me pick out some silverware. It was important to me to have some nice silverware in our home, and I wanted to register for it so our friends who were looking for a gift idea would know what to get. But Dwight couldn't have cared less. And he kept poking me in the store, telling me so. I was getting more upset by the minute, but he just kept on. Finally, I could take it no more.

"Just take me home," I told him. I cried all the way there, then went to my room and cried some more.

Although I really didn't care about the silverware, I guess I could have been a little more congenial about it. But I got upset too. In fact, I was so mad I probably would not have ever called Deb again. I don't think she would have called me, either, because she could be pretty headstrong also. Fortunately, Deb's mom got on the phone the next morning and did some calling herself.

"Dwight," she said. "You better get over here and work this out." I was almost relieved when she called, because I wasn't about to take the first step. She then went to Deb's room and informed her that I was coming over. Needless to say, Deb wasn't the least bit pleased.

"But I don't want to see him," she wailed.

"Well, you have to," her mother replied. So we talked it out, and we're so glad we did. Deb's mom gave me some good advice that day.

"Listen, Dwight," she said. "All work and no play makes Jack a dull boy. You have to stop and smell the roses."

"Well, my name isn't Jack and I'm not dull," I shot back. But in my heart I knew she was right. I was always working and not getting much sleep, making me more stressed out. And I did try to change.

Some of the arguments we had during our engagement really bothered me. I saw so many marriages failing around us. And I didn't want to be like that. It frustrated me when I got angry with Deb, too. I wanted to be like Jesus, to find something that worked and have a happy home. But at that point in my life, I just didn't know how.

We certainly don't recommend early marriages to anyone who might be considering it. But in the end we were married, and it was a very happy day in my life.

Gems of Thought

As I look back on everything now, I can clearly see how God was leading in this situation. He knew exactly what I needed and how Deb would be just the one for my character. He also knew my future and how Deb would fit into it.

14

Off With a "Bang"

I wish I could say that our first year together was filled with sunsets and roses. But to be perfectly honest, we were incredibly busy. For starters, I was still a senior in high school. So I attended school until 3 p.m. everyday, then hurried to work at a nearby daycare center.

Although I got off work at 6 every night, my day was far from over. In the evenings I would help Dwight build our house, and we worked late—often until 2 a.m. Of course, building our own home was a lot of work. It could also be rather frustrating. When we started, I didn't even know what a penny nail was. But I learned my "nails and tools" very quickly—because I had to.

It was during our home building project that I was first introduced, and I mean really introduced, to Dwight's bad temper. It all started one night when we were trying to put up drywall on the second floor.

I had been carrying sheets of drywall upstairs all by myself, and I was dead tired. Upstairs in the bedroom, I had built a "T" from two-by-fours that was doubling as a drywall lift. So I would lift the drywall over my head, sweating and pushing for all I was worth, while Deb "kicked" the bottom side of the "T." Once the "T" was in place, I could put in some nails and relax a bit. But until that moment, holding the drywall in place took every ounce of energy I could muster.

I was not only tired, but also super stressed. Every morning I woke up at 4:30 a.m. and got to work by 5:00 a.m. Anyone in construction knows it is hard work. I would get home around 6:00 p.m., eat some supper, and start working on my house. Daryl, my best friend, would get out of work at 11:00 p.m. and then come over to help me. We would work 'til 2:00 a.m., and then the cycle would start all over again. Little did I realize my problem. Since I was not connected with Christ, I took my frustrations out on my wife.

I was trying to be helpful, but it didn't seem like Dwight was very patient with me.

"Kick it! Kick it!" he yelled as he sweated and strained to hold this one particular piece in its place.

"I AM kicking it!" I shouted back.

"No! You're just tapping!"

"I'm kicking!"

"NO! You're tapping! You have to kick it!" The argument would have gone on and on, except Dwight couldn't hold that piece up any longer. There was a thunderous sound as it hit the floor. The drywall was ruined, and it was all my fault (or so Dwight thought), and he totally lost it. His temper, that is. He was so angry, he started beating that piece of drywall with his hammer. I wasn't sure what to think. Unfortunately, this was the first of many times I would see Dwight lose his temper.

I didn't want to lose my temper like that, of course. But I hadn't surrendered my heart to the Lord, so I didn't handle those frustrations very well. And we were so stressed out, right from the get-go.

I knew I could continue to make excuses like "I'm tired and stressed," or "I got my temper honestly because my dad had a real problem with his temper." I could just say I was born with it, I can't help it. I had even heard pastors say some of these problems we are born with and are within us and we can't change. It was true that I had never been taught to leave my temper with Christ in a practical way. It was only by theory that I knew. Yet deep down I knew that I could give it to the Lord. he could give me the power to gain the victory. I longed for someone to help me.

In building our home, we soon found that our tastes differed on a number of items. I wanted a green countertop, and she wanted another color. We couldn't even agree on curtains.

Sometimes Deb would suggest that I put a door here, or there, or do something different on the house. Having grown up around construction all my life, I basically knew what could and couldn't be done. But Deb had no concept of what was going on.

"Boy, that's pretty stupid," was my standard reply to many of her suggestions. And then we would get into an argument. Part of the problem was that self—not Christ—was the foundation of our marriage.

Being a newlywed, a high school senior, and builder's assistant wasn't that easy. Sometimes my "jobs" as a wife conflicted with my "duties" as a student. For example, one time Dwight wanted me to be at home when the electricians came to wire the house.

"You need to tell them a few things for me," Dwight said.

"I can't, Dwight," I replied. "I really can't miss any school."

"Call the school" Dwight suggested.

"Deb Hall won't be in today," I said, in my most convincing voice.

"Who's calling please?" The secretary on the other end of the line wanted to know.

"This is Mrs. Hall," I said, and of course, that was no lie.

"OK, fine," said the secretary, but Dwight didn't like my methods.

In spite of our somewhat bumpy ride that first year, I did manage to finish high school about the same time we were finishing the house. In fact, we even had the house carpeted in time for my high school graduation.

You'd think that working, studying, building a marriage relationship and a house would have been enough for us to tackle that first year. But we had another project in the works as well, which would affect our lives for years to come.

Gems of Thought

Since I was not connected with Christ, I took my frustrations out on my wife.

All of us are born with deficiencies. It is so easy to make excuses for them. For me it was my temper, and from the beginning I nurtured it weekly, until it was just part of my life. When we connect to Christ good changes will come.

15

Building a Business

In addition to building a house, I also started my own business during our first year of marriage. Being a car and truck buff, I chose to sell "aftermarket" auto accessories (like fancy shock absorbers) to soup up 4-wheel drive trucks. Off road vehicles were a big thing at that time, and our company sold suspension systems, shocks, roll bars and other accessories for the growing market.

I started Hall's Off-road Equipment on a shoestring, so during the start-up I did double duty at the construction company to make ends meet. My younger brother Dan, who was still in high school, worked with me right from the start.

On a usual day, I got up at four or five in the morning to get things ready for the construction crew. Then I returned to the business to order parts and handle the business end of my store.

Since we couldn't afford to hire a mechanic, I also installed the suspension systems myself—in the evening. I usually grabbed a bite to eat around 10 p.m., and then worked on the house until two or three in the morning. In case you haven't figured it out already, during this time I only got 1 or 2 hours of sleep each night. And I needed all the help I could get from Deb, although once again she ran into some conflicts between her jobs as student and helpful wife.

One day Dwight wanted me to run to the bank

69

between classes and make a deposit.

"I just can't do it, Dwight," I told him. I only had a 5-minute break between classes—not nearly enough time to run to the bank and back.

"But you really have to," Dwight argued. "This money has to go in the bank tomorrow, that's all there is to it." He couldn't do the banking himself, because he had to be on the road supervising a construction crew.

Now, I didn't want to have an unexcused absence. But I also didn't see how I could get it excused. For starters, I had never told the school I was married! And they weren't in the habit of excusing students to go to the bank.

In the end, I decided to go the principal's office, tell him exactly what I needed to do, and ask if I could quickly run my errand.

"Absolutely not," the principal had no intention of letting me go. "I'll have a teacher at every door if necessary, but you're staying here."

I knew Dwight was depending on me, so after a rather lengthy discussion I turned to my strategy of last resort.

"My husband will be very upset with you if you don't allow me to go to the bank," I informed the principal. I'll never forget the look on his face.

"You're married?"

"Yes," I informed him. "Would you like to speak with my husband about this?"

"OK," the principal agreed. We placed a phone call to Dwight, who was indeed upset. In the end, the principal let me go to the bank.

Hall's Off-road Equipment continued to grow and prosper, so my brother Rudy opened up a second store in Traverse City, Michigan. Within six months, business was going so well that my brother

Building a Business

Dan and I decided to start manufacturing our own suspension products. The new manufacturing operation, which we named Trailmaster, also did extremely well. Within several years, the company grew to be the second largest aftermarket suspension company for 4-wheel drives in the world.

I guess being young has its advantages and disadvantages. When we first started Trailmaster, my competitors in the auto industry didn't take us very seriously. I was still in my early twenties, and Dan was still in his teens. We both looked like two young kids, barely able to drive. I was also new to the industry so other businesspeople didn't spend too much time with me at the trade shows. All that changed as Trailmaster continued to grow and prosper.

Getting a business off the ground while building a house was hard work, but Deb and I did accomplish a lot that first year of marriage. Unfortunately, none of my accomplishments were spiritual in nature. I knew that I was what people called "the American dream" —having it all. But why wasn't I happy? Something was missing. What was it?

Gems of Thought

I knew that I was living what people called "the American dream"—having it all. But why wasn't I happy? Something was missing. What was it?

16

Still Something Missing

Somehow I felt that getting married, building a home, and starting my own business would all help to "settle me down." And it's just like that with so many people today. If they can just "get out of debt," "put in a swimming pool," "buy a new car" or "learn one more truth," maybe then life will be all they hoped it would be. And so I kept adding to my plate of responsibilities, thinking that if I just did "one more thing," I would automatically stop partying and grow closer to Jesus.

But unfortunately, while the exterior parts of my life were changing, my heart was not. In spite of my marriage, new home, and growing business, I was the same beer-drinking party lover I had been for so long. Some nights I would come home late to find Deb still up, waiting for me.

"Dwight," she would plead, "why were you out drinking with the guys? You could have spent time with me. After all, we're married!"

"Honey, you just don't understand," I often replied. "I really do love you. But I work all week, and this is my way to relax. It's just a social thing—me and the guys."

"But Dwight, what's wrong with me?" she would ask. "Why don't you want to spend this time with me?"

"Nothing is wrong with you," I retorted. To which she would say, "Well, there must be, if whenever we have free time you just want to be with the guys."

Still Something Missing

After we got married, I didn't understand the change in Dwight's drinking habits. While we were dating, he didn't "go out with the guys." At that point, his drinking consisted of sharing a beer or two with my dad in the evenings. But after our marriage, Dwight started going out to pick up beer with some of his friends. Then sometimes they would just drive around and drink, or come home and play cards.

One time when I was disgusted with Dwight for drinking so much, I asked him if I could have the refunds from his beer cans to use as I wished. I figured if he was going to drink beer, I might as well get something out of it, too.

Well, as you can imagine, that refund money added up. So much so, in fact, that I would buy myself a new dress every few months just with the refund money!

Then Dwight would get mad at me, because we were still starting up the business and things were very tight.

"Where'd you get the money to buy a new dress?" he wanted to know.

"From the beer can money," I would sweetly reply. And he couldn't say any more, because he had told me I could have that money. And he could have reduced my wardrobe allowance at any time, by reducing his drinking.

I couldn't believe it when Deb actually started buying new dresses with my beer can money. For one thing, most of my drinking was out with the guys. I usually didn't bring home my beer cans, and I tried not to drink at home. So when Deb asked me if she could have my beer can money, I said, "Sure." I didn't figure it would amount to much anyway. But when she started buying dresses with that money, I knew the problem was bigger than I wanted to admit. And it bugged me, because our finances were really tight and here she was out buying a new outfit. Of course, Deb could have argued that I was spending way too much on beer if she could buy a dress from my bottle returns, and she was right.

As time went on, things started to get more and more out of hand. One night when we were planning to play cards, Dwight and my brother Randy wanted a six-pack of beer. So they drove out to get it, saying they would be right back.

While they were gone, I kept on playing cards with my sister-in-law. And every now and then we would see Dwight's jeep start to come down the lane toward our house, but then he would turn around and go back. I didn't know what was going on then, but I certainly found out later. Dwight and Randy drank the first six-pack before they ever got home. As they were turning down the lane toward our house, they decided to go back and get another one, which they did.

Unfortunately, they managed to guzzle that six-pack down before they got home. Once again, they turned down the lane toward our home before deciding to go back for more.

I'm not for sure how many six-packs they drank that night, or how many times they headed back to get more, but it was far too many. When Dwight finally did get home, it was very late. And he was drunk, incredibly drunk.

Now as you can imagine, anybody who drinks that much beer will most certainly find their way to the bathroom, or at least try, during the night. And I don't want to say too much about this, but when a mind is in that kind of a drunken condition it must be very easy to mix up the bathroom and a windowsill. That's what Dwight did anyway, and to be perfectly honest, I was totally disgusted. And for the first time in our life together, I realized that he really did have a problem with drinking.

When I sobered up that morning and Deb showed me what I had done, I could hardly believe it.

"Dwight, you ought to stop drinking," Deb said. But although I was disgusted with myself, I didn't like Deb telling me what to do.

"Well, I work hard," I snapped back. "I deserve a drink now and then."

But in my heart I knew something was wrong. It seemed like all the "pieces" of the American dream were falling into place for me. And my friends were saying, "Man, you are so lucky." I had a wonderful wife, nice home, and thriving business—yet I was still running here and there, trying to fill the empty void in my life. In my heart I knew that something was still missing. I was learning the hard way that marriage, money, a home and even a semblance of worldly happiness could not buy the peace that I wanted so badly.

I kept looking for the externals, and I had one more last ditch effort to take care of my drinking and other problems. This plan had to work.

Gems of Thought

Like the world and most Christians, we keep putting our trust and so-called happiness in things. It is the "if only" syndrome, or "I'll get to it", or especially "I don't see what's so bad about this." Like myself, many of us keep our eyes focused on others for good or for bad. It's either "If only I could have what they have" or "Look at them, see what they are doing, I'm not really that bad." If we would just focus on the One who can take care of all these problems, we would be so much happier.

17

The American Dream

After Deb and I were married about two and a half years, we had a baby girl. She was such a beautiful child, and we named her Alysha. This is it, I thought. This will help me settle down. This is the key to my happiness.

Unfortunately, during the early years of Alysha's life I still drank and went out with the guys as much as I always did. In my sober moments, I realized that marriage, home ownership, and now becoming a parent had all failed to "settle me down." But still I insisted on looking outside myself to root up the unhappiness I felt inside.

So I threw myself all the more wholeheartedly into our business, and it grew by leaps and bounds. And it had to, from my perspective, because I couldn't stand the thought of failure. In fact, I had promised myself several years earlier that I would never fail again.

As Trailmaster became more and more successful, we decided to add a second location in Tulsa, Oklahoma. Tulsa was ideal for shipping because of its central location. In addition, labor was plentiful and relatively inexpensive.

So Deb and I decided to move to Tulsa, start up the new manufacturing plant, and in the process, maybe even have a new start for us.

This success we achieved was not without effect. People

noticed, and continued to say I was living the "American Dream." They respected me, and my old school friends thought I was lucky. As for myself, I was so happy not to be a failure. At last, I was somebody.

I was excited about moving to Oklahoma. It was rewarding to watch Trailmaster grow, and I also hoped that Dwight would cut down on his drinking when we moved.

Unfortunately, things did not turn out as I had hoped. While in Coldwater, Dwight had become really good friends with a guy named Brad. The two of them spent a lot of time together working on the Jeep that Dwight owned, and they drank a lot together.

Some nights when Brad and I were out cruising around together, we would stop to look up at the stars, kind of like I used to do when I was in the army. Brad would say to me, "Do you really think there is a God?"

"Yes, I know there's a God," I would tell him. That would start our debates on the subject. I was always trying to convince Brad that there was a God, and that there was also a "right" and a "wrong." Brad wasn't so sure if he believed me, but we were the best of friends anyway.

When I went down to Tulsa a month before Deb did to start up the business, Brad came along to help. We opened a Hall's Off-road Store down there, and in our spare time, we drank.

One night, after we had been in Tulsa for two or three weeks, something happened that profoundly affected my life. Brad and I had been out to a bar that night, drinking, so when the phone rang at 7 a.m., I was still a little bit groggy.

"Dwight, I have some terrible news," I heard the voice of my father say on the other end of the line. "There was a bad accident last night, and Scott was killed."

Scott was my cousin, a few years younger than I and engaged

to be married in about two weeks. In addition to being my cousin, Scott was a very good friend of mine. We grew up together, played on the same basketball team. Scott had been out with the guys for a stag party when the Corvette he was in rolled over, landing on top of him. So when I got that horrible message on the phone that morning, I couldn't believe my ears. By the time I got off the phone I was shaking uncontrollably.

I thought of the time, just a few weeks ago, when I had been back in Coldwater. I had been out late with the guys. As usual, I was drinking and driving my souped-up Jeep. And we were cruising, listening to my tremendous stereo system and flying down the road at speeds between 110 and 120 miles per hour.

"It should have been me," I kept saying to myself, over and over again. "I was out partying last night, too, and I've been drinking a lot longer than Scott ever did." I wondered why I had escaped the night Scott died. And I wondered about Scott, how he stood with God, and what it was like to have your probation suddenly finished. For the first time in a while, I started thinking very seriously about my life.

But while I wanted to be a Christian, I still felt confused about it all. I knew that if I really gave myself to Jesus, I would put everything into it. Because that's the type of person I am. I had always been hard on "fake" Christians, who seemed to keep all the rules and regulations not because they enjoyed it, but because they felt they had to.

"If I surrender myself to Christ, will it take all the joy out of my life? Will I be sad all the time, or can Christianity actually be a blessing?" I wondered. "Is it possible to enjoy being a Christian?"

I understood that all the rules and regulations were supposed to be for my benefit, not my detriment. However, when I looked around me I didn't see any Christians who looked like they were having any fun, unless they were acting just like the world. I saw plenty of those type of "Christians"—in name only. And some of the ones who "kept the rules" were drinking or smoking or cheating on their taxes.

The American Dream

All along, I knew what I was doing was wrong. It was obvious. But I didn't want to play church. Where is someone who can show, not just talk, Christianity? Please God, I would cry out. Where?

It is really strange, but that still small voice would speak to me and say, "Don't look to others. Look to Me. I am your Example."

I didn't want to be a legalist who kept the law and didn't enjoy it, but I also didn't believe in a "do-nothing" religion.

"Where are the Christians?" I wondered. I was so afraid to take the step myself for fear that I would either be miserable, or become just like others, a selective Christian which to me was no Christian at all.

It was during this time that I had another embarrassing "drinking experience." It happened in California, while I was traveling on business for Trailmaster. Brad and I had gone out that night, and once again I was really drunk.

During the night when I got up to use the restroom, I accidentally went through the wrong door. Which is how I found myself, in my underwear, standing alone in the hallway of a Marriott Inn. Before I figured out what was going on, the door had closed behind me and I was locked out. Even in my inebriated state it was all rather embarrassing, so I scrunched in the doorway and tried knocking softly on the door so as not to wake up anyone but Brad.

Now, Brad was asleep in the room. But he was also dead drunk, and I couldn't raise him for anything. It was the middle of the night, but at that moment I honestly didn't care. I stopped tapping and pounded on that door for all I was worth. During all this time my roommate never did wake up, but I must have woken up somebody because pretty soon an elevator door opened and out walked a security guard.

"What are you doing out here?" he wanted to know.

"I'm just standing here, for the fun of it," I snapped. As you can see I'm locked out of my room."

"Not a problem. I can let you in just as soon as you show me some identification," he replied.

"Oh right," I said sarcastically, looking down at my shorts. "As if I have my wallet with me."

In the end he let me in, and then I showed him my identification. Of course, Brad woke up and wanted to know what was going on the minute we opened the door.

"Why didn't you hear me?" I yelled. "I pounded on this door for twenty minutes!"

I was mad at Brad, mad at the hotel, and mad at the world. But most of all I was mad at myself, and that night was a turning point in my life. I had admitted I had a drinking problem before, but now, for the first time, I began to seriously consider what I could do about it. And for me, that was very significant.

Why is it we have to get so low before we give Christ a real try? In John 14:6 it says, "I am the way, the truth, and the life: no man cometh unto the Father, but by me." Christ really does have the way out for us.

At this point in time, I was not yet through fighting with God. I wanted Him so bad, yet was so scared. Another lesson was in the works.

Gems of Thought

The Bible says if you keep the whole law and stumble in one point, you break all the law. (James 2:10) "For this is the love of God, that we keep his commandments: and his commandments are not grievous (1 John 5:3). I could go on and on with texts. Why is it we have to get so low before we give Christ a real try? In John 14:6 it says, "I am the way, the truth, and the life: no man cometh unto the Father, but by me."

18

Riding the Fence

About a year after we moved to Tulsa, we hired a man named Bill to work for Trailmaster. Bill was a really nice guy—hard working and intelligent, and he and Dwight hit it off right away. Even I felt pretty positive about their relationship. Since Bill was twice as old as Dwight (they were 50 and 25 years old, respectively), I thought maybe Bill would be a good influence; maybe even settle Dwight down. But unfortunately, things didn't work out that way. All too soon, it was the same old story but with a different friend, for Dwight and Bill had become real drinking buddies, a real heartbreak for me.

Bill wasn't a Christian, but he knew something about Seventh-day Adventists. And he wanted nothing to do with them. There was something different about Dwight, however, and (from a Christian point of view) it wasn't exactly a positive thing.

"You know, Dwight," Bill used to say after the two of them had shared a drink. "For an Adventist, you're all right!" It really bothered Dwight whenever Bill made that comment. In his heart, he knew he wasn't a very good example of what a Christian should be.

Things didn't go that smoothly during our three

years in Tulsa. Although the business continued to grow and prosper, Dwight had to handle a lot of personnel problems at the office. It seemed we were always having trouble with workers. In fact, in one year, Dwight had to let go of twenty-five employees. Needless to say, he was under a lot of stress.

During all this time I stayed home with Alysha. It was Dwight's job to take care of the business, and I took care of our home. But one day when Dwight came home I could tell he was really bothered about something.

"Deb, I need some help," he said, referring to the employment situation in the office.

"Well, get some help," I told him.

"You don't understand, Deb," he said. "I really need somebody in the office."

"Then get somebody in the office," I told him again.

"But I need someone I can really depend on," Dwight said.

"Then find her!" I replied.

Well, to make a long story short, Dwight did "find her." And "she" was me. I started work at Trailmaster the next morning.

During all this time Dwight was still drinking with Bill. Although he was still the same hard working and responsible man I had married, and although we were attending a church, we were very much "on the fence" spiritually. Dwight especially was struggling with all of this.

"Either I'm going to do the religion thing, or I'm not," he told me. He was tired of living contrary to his beliefs, of being a half-baked Christian.

I should have been happy, but I wasn't. After all this, something was still missing. I was not at peace with myself. Many times, my mind went back to the words of a song I knew in high school that said something about "dying to live and living to die." And I wondered, why am I dying to live? Is there more to life than this? Or am I just living to die?

As I look back on it now, I realize the Holy Spirit was working nonstop on my conscience. There was a "still small voice" in my life, and it was saying to me:

"Dwight, you have got to make a decision. Either you are for me or against me. It doesn't matter if you are rich and travel the world over for your business. It doesn't even matter how many children you have. What really matters is if you are right with God. And Dwight, you have got to make a decision."

I felt this struggle to the core of my heart. For so many years I had resisted a full commitment because I didn't want to be a fake or failure. But it was time—time for me to take a stand.

In my heart, I knew that I was successful in my business because I was willing to make it succeed. When it came to achieving success, I would work all night if I had to. But the question that kept haunting my soul was this: Was I willing to make that level of commitment to God?

God is so good. During the time that I was struggling, the church held an evangelistic series. While I had hated going to those meetings when I was a kid, I felt moved to go. I had been to so many that I had been burned out. Yet, I felt compelled to go. I was so compelled that I even asked Bill who was still living with us because his house had not yet sold in Michigan, and his wife Arlene was there trying to sell it. He surprised me by saying he would go to one meeting.

A few weeks later on Sabbath afternoon, a few hours before the meetings were to begin, I was engaged in my usual round of "lay activities" (e.g. sacked out on the couch). But for some odd reason I just couldn't sleep. Usually I had no problem sleeping the afternoon away after working all kinds of hours. The week always exhausted me. Today, I could not sleep. That bothered me since Sabbath was just a big bore. A voice in my head kept saying, "Dwight. Go remind Bill that the meeting starts tonight." Bill and Arlene had just sold their home, and their furniture and belongings had just arrived on Wednesday evening. We had helped them move all their belongings into the house.

But I just lay there tossing and turning, overcome by this very real conviction that I should remind Bill of the evangelistic series that night. Now this was an unusual thought for me. To top it all off, Bill and Arlene had just moved on Wednesday. Knowing first-hand that their house was in a shambles, I didn't see how I could possibly invite them to attend a meeting that night. That voice was very strong in my head. I had no idea the Holy Spirit was trying to reach me. No one in all my years of church going had explained to me that still small voice. God loved me. Even in this condition He loved me. What a God we serve.

Finally, I could stand it no longer. "I'm going to get up and go see Bill," I told Deb.

"Fine," she nodded. "I'll wake up Alysha and go, too."

"No," I refused. "I want to go by myself."

When I got to Bill's, it was still a terrible mess. To make matters worse, he was having trouble getting his refrigerator to run. But being his usual congenial self, he offered me a beer and I drank it. Then I got right to the point. I didn't figure Bill would come anyway, but at the very least, I could ease my troubled conscience.

"Bill," I started. "I've decided to go to these religious meetings tonight. Would you like to come along?"

That was the last straw for Arlene, who blew up at both of us.

"We're not going to any religious meetings," she pointed an angry finger in Bill's direction. "You need to get this refrigerator fixed Bill. We don't even have our bed set up yet."

Strangely enough, I was almost relieved at her response. "You see," I said to myself. "That was stupid to ask anyway. You knew all along that they weren't going to go, so why did you even ask?"

I was quiet then, which is very unusual for me. But I was thinking of my own spiritual experience, and how badly I needed to go to those meetings. Then Bill turned to his wife.

"I did tell Dwight I would like to go with him to one meeting," he said.

"Yeah, you need to go to the first night so you don't miss something," I blurted out. Then I asked Arlene if Bill could go if I helped fix the refrigerator that afternoon. In the end, she said OK, and even came to the meeting herself, although somewhat grudgingly.

Something happened to me that day when I talked with Bill by his refrigerator. I guess I had finally decided that if I was really going to change, I had better start doing it. And that beer Bill handed me—it was the last beer I ever drank.

Now, I don't want anyone to think that quitting was really that easy. I know the Lord does take the desire for beer from some people, but that didn't happen to me. I really missed my beer, because I had liked it so well. In fact, I had nightmares about alcohol for the next five years, but praise God I was victorious. I won that victory in His strength.

As for Bill and Arlene, they seemed to enjoy the first meeting, so they went to another, and another. In fact, they made it to almost every meeting.

In spite of Bill's former aversion to Christianity, he was a real Bible student. At one point in his life he had studied the Bible in depth. He even believed that Jesus was coming very soon. Unfortunately, he made a very significant mistake: Bill set a date when he felt Jesus would come. Evidently he missed the text in the Bible that says, "But of that day and hour knoweth no man, no, not the angels of heaven, but my Father only" (Matthew 24:36).

When Jesus didn't come at Bill's projected time, he became very upset. So upset, in fact, that he threw all his Bibles and commentaries away.

"I don't ever want to hear the word of God spoken again," he told his family. He meant it, too. But something changed for Bill during those evangelistic meetings, and it also happened for me. We became very excited about what we were hearing, and started meeting every night to study the Bible in even more depth.

During the first meeting, the evangelist spoke about the soon-coming end of the world. While I had heard about the "shortness of time" all my life, it hit me that night like a ton of bricks. I made up my mind to attend all the meetings, and not miss a single one. So I went five nights a week for five weeks, and to my surprise, wasn't the least bit bored. In fact, I was eager to go.

For so many years I had wondered if it was even possible to be a real Christian. But as I attended the meetings, the little seed of hope started to grow within my heart. I knew that this was the time for me to make a decision, to get off the fence and be a real Christian.

"But is it really possible for me—Dwight Hall—to truly walk with God?" I wondered in my heart. "Can I really walk with God?" I was still so afraid of becoming a hypocrite; yet there was this yearning in my heart, this incredible longing. I soon began to believe that, with Jesus' help, I could actually walk with God.

Gems of Thought

As I look back on it now, I realize the Holy Spirit was working nonstop on my conscience. Many times I thought I would surrender my heart to God "soon." But God in His mercy showed me that if I kept delaying, "soon" would never come. ". . .Behold, now is the accepted time; behold, now is the day of salvation" (2 Corinthians 6:2). Soon is like a mirage. It is always just in front of you, but no matter how much you hope and desire, without a conscious decision, you will never get to it.

19

A Turning Point

I don't fully know how to explain this, but things started coming together for Dwight and I during that evangelistic series. For the first time in my life, I started to really understand that there were reasons behind the rules. And I came to know Jesus like I had never known Him before—to love Him as my personal Savior.

I don't mean to discount my spiritual experience when, as a teenager I gave my heart to Jesus and was baptized. I did go through two sets of Bible studies at that time, and thought I understood. But this time, everything became so real to me. Jesus was real, and He was alive, and I wanted to love and serve Him for the rest of my life.

At the end of the evangelistic series, I made a new commitment to Jesus. I bought myself a new Bible and held it up, promising to read it consistently. I said, "I will read and study this even if it is one of the most boring books I have ever read." I wanted to study God's word for myself, and see how true it was. I've kept that promise ever since.

At the end of the evangelistic series, Bill and Arlene were both baptized. As for Deb and myself, we rededicated our lives to the Lord, and as we did, things started to change in our lives.

Learning to Walk With God

Before our newly found Christian experience, we used to play cards with Bill and Arlene every Saturday night. In academy I could never understand why playing with regular playing cards was wrong but it was OK to play UNO. So I played cards for years. But when I started reading my Bible, it hit me that just "blowing my time" while in the midst of a lost and dying world was wrong. Deb, Bill and Arlene became convicted of the same thing at about the same time. So we just quit playing cards. And I haven't played or wanted to play cards since. We just decided that time was short, and that we wanted to spend our time living and loving what Jesus wanted us to do. We started to realize that we all have only two reasons for living:

- to develop a character like our example, Jesus, and
- to share our experiences with others.

All these other things became distractions.

As we continued to read our Bibles, Deb and I also made the decision to get out of debt. Until then, we had been just like a lot of other people who blow their money as fast as it comes in. But we read in the Bible where it says you should "owe no man anything" . Romans 13:8. Also we read the text where it said "The rich ruleth over the poor, and the borrower is servant to the lender." So we decided to reduce our expenses one by one. For example, we got rid of cable TV. We also replaced our car with a less expensive model we could pay cash for. Then we ripped up our credit cards and started paying tithe. Up until this time, we had never paid tithe consistently because we never had the money. As we started cutting our expenses and doing what God asked us to do, we found that we had money to pay tithe and some to spare.

Paying tithe was a real step in faith for me, for I wasn't used to trusting in a power outside of myself. But Deb and I chose to step out in faith—without seeing. When you are so used to making things happen yourself, it is very difficult to turn things over. But I said I would trust in God and live by His word. I believed, and still do believe, that His word is not old-fashioned. For God is not just history, but future also. He would never give me something old and out of date.

So we decided to pay a "tithe" to ourselves as well. In other words, after giving a tithe, 10%, plus a 5% offering and freewill offering, to the Lord, we put another 10% in the savings account. Pretty soon we had $100 in the savings account. And believe me, that was a real milestone for us. Up to this time in our lives we had never made much money. I always thought that if I could just make more money I would be able to get out of debt. We began to understand the Scripture about owing no man anything—that it wasn't more money but living within our means that would free us from debt.

Many times I had heard Malachi 3:8-10 read and expounded in church. The words that always caught my ears and interest were "prove Me now in this, says the Lord of hosts, if I will not open for you the windows of heaven and pour out for you such blessing that there will not be room enough to receive it." My thoughts were always "OK, Lord, pour that money down from the sky so I can get my bills paid. Then give me a double portion so I can have money in the bank. Don't worry Lord—I will also pay you some extra to help with the mission field or whatever. In my quiet time I realized that as my heart drew closer to God, He was once again trying to get me to see His principles. "Dwight," He seemed to say. "I own the cattle upon a thousand hills." Psalms 50:10 "Don't you know that 'All the earth is mine.'" Exodus 19:5. "It's not your money I need, but your entire heart." Deb and I found that when we put these principles to work with a contrite heart, we would have a blessing we would not be able to receive. I can tell you it works. By getting rid of the unnecessary things in our life like the new car, cable TV, etc., we found that we had more spendable income. It didn't stop there, either. By having an older auto, our insurance was less. Can you begin to see the great possibilities?

We also saved money by consulting each other on financial decisions, and waiting one week before we bought anything. Many times we found that once a week had passed by, we didn't need anything so bad after all. If one of us did still want the item after a week, then we would discuss it, pray about it, and make a decision together. And we started making the Bible the foundation of our financial decisions. Instead of saying "I don't see anything wrong with this," we asked, "what would Jesus do?" And that question alone really changed our buying patterns.

During this incredible time of change in our lives, we also added another beautiful baby girl to our family. We named her Natysha, and of course, we were very happy at her arrival.

As I continued to grow in my spiritual experience, there was born in my heart a desire to be rebaptized. Although I had been baptized at age 14 when I was in academy, I hadn't really realized what it was all about at that time. As a result, I did what so many have done both before and after me: I was "buried alive". In other words, I kept my sins in my back pocket buried deep within me and brought them back up with me again, instead of dying to my sins as I was supposed to do.

A short time after my re-conversion, an evangelist led a trip to Israel, which is home to so many historic Biblical places. Deb and I arranged to go on this trip along with other friends and family members. There, in the Jordan River, where Jesus had been baptized, we had the special privilege of rededicating our lives to Him in this special way. The water was icy, but my heart was warm inside—warm with love for Jesus and the joy of knowing Him as my personal Lord and Savior.

My rebaptism meant so much more than the first time around. Not that it has to be that way—but this time, I understood that baptism meant death to self and a new life in Christ. Jesus was going to live in me! I could die to self daily by depending on Jesus and walking with Him every step of the way.

The Bible speaks of baptism as a "burial." When a person is dead, they do not respond to anything. And when I am dead to sin in Christ, I do not respond to sin. This does not mean my sinful nature hasn't tried to "rise again" since I was baptized. Paul said "I die daily," 1 Corinthians 15:31 meaning that he fought this battle and won it, in the strength of Jesus, every day.

For the first time I understood what being baptized under the water really meant. It was paralleling a death. When you die you are completely buried. What a representation. It is also important that we be old enough to know what this really means.

So many of us are what I call "buried alive." We go down into the watery grave and come back up the same as before. That is why I believe God asks us to do things a certain way. God is so loving and so merciful that He wants to give us every advantage He can. These so-called little things in life make a big difference. We should never think we are wiser than God. If we do, we become like Adam and Eve by thinking this is no big deal. It is only a piece of fruit. When we start getting the idea that little things don't make us or break us, we fall right onto Satan's enchanted ground. Whenever I start to think this way, I remember the first part of Luke 16:10: "He that is faithful in that which is least is faithful also in much." Anyone who has ever been in charge of people knows what I am talking about. It is the little things that trip us up.

When I was a teenager, I didn't understand what it meant to die to sin. I believed in "life after death." I didn't come up a new creature or person in Christ, so there was no significant change in me. But praise God, this time I saw what it meant to give my all—my whole life to Christ. Through His power, I was thrilled to "bury" my sins under the water.

The first communion I took part in after my baptism also had a very special meaning for me. It was actually Bill who really explained the true significance of this service to me.

"Do you know what I'm doing, Dwight?" he asked me while washing my feet.

"Yeah, Bill, you're washing my feet," I replied.

"But Dwight," he said, and there were tears in his eyes, "do you realize the significance of this?" I was quiet for a minute, thinking, so he went on. "Dwight, I'm washing your feet, and that's a dirty job. Who would want to wash somebody's feet? But look what Christ did!"

Then we talked some more about what it really meant to be a servant—to wash somebody else's feet. And what had been just a tradition to me before, suddenly took on a whole new meaning. In time, I also came to understand that the foot washing ceremony in communion is also a rebaptism experience. I learned from the Bible that at first, Peter didn't want Jesus to wash his feet. After all, Jesus was his Lord and Master. It wasn't until Jesus told Peter that He had to wash Peter's feet or Peter wouldn't be clean that the disciple changed his tune. Then, being the impetuous "all-or-nothing" guy that he was, he asked Jesus to not just wash his feet, but also all of him! But Jesus told him that foot washing was sufficient (John 13:5-10).

There were many more wonderful Bible insights I gained both during this time, and since. And while much of what I learned was directly from the Bible itself, I came to understand much more about Jesus through reading the *Bible Study Companion Set* (the set which we now sell so many of in our ministry today). One of the books in this set, *The Desire of Ages*, tells the story of Jesus' life and sacrifice in such an incredible and moving way. When I read that, I realized more fully what Jesus really did for me on the cross. I was inspired to study my Bible even more, digging deeper than ever into the truths of God's word. The Bible says, "Faith cometh by hearing, and hearing by the Word of God" (Romans 10:17). As I searched God's Word for myself, I was beginning to find the peace I needed so badly.

During this time, the Bible became very real to me. In fact, I stopped reading all books but the Bible and the *Bible Study Companion Set*. Every new truth I found, I tried to incorporate into my daily life. The gospel became practical to me. At last, the future looked truly rosy. For the first time in my life, I felt that I really did "have it all."

A Turning Point

Gems of Thought

God has called His people—real Christians—to be the light of the world (Matthew 5:14). Then we are a special people (1 Peter 2:9). We have a great responsibility as well as a tremendous opportunity, like being in the special forces. As Deb and I share with you our experiences, we do not in the least think that you need to do what we did, in any way or in any order. You need to look at the principles that we share.

We will continue to tell how God worked in our life. Again this is not about some denomination. It's about learning to walk with God. We just ask that you be honest and open to the Lord. As He becomes the Lord of your life, you will find it becomes easier to follow your convictions.

20

Eating to Live

During this incredible time of change in our lives, Deb and I also began studying how we could have healthier bodies. The changes we made in our diet before Alysha was born had nothing to do with religion: we just wanted to have a healthy child.

When Deb was pregnant for Alysha, we saw a special documentary on television. The documentary was made in Michigan not far from where we lived. It showed how the cattle, especially the milking cows, were becoming deformed. It was because of the chemicals the cattle were getting. Then it showed many calves were dying at birth, if not before. That was bad enough, but it didn't end there. Many of the calves that lived were deformed. Worst of all, the documentary said that some human babies were even dying from the milk. At the end of the program it alerted the women that were pregnant not to drink milk—at least not during their pregnancy. That got our attention. I am not one to make a hasty decision, especially on this topic since I still ate a tremendous amount of meat and drank at least two to four gallons of milk myself a week. I decided to go to some bookstores and read up on this so-called problem. What I found shook me up to say the least. With Deb soon to have our first child and not wanting to have anything wrong with it, we decided to quit drinking milk and eating red meat.

Eating to Live

Often Dwight would sit down and open up a book to read after supper. One night, after he had picked up one of those books he suddenly became very angry. Slamming the book shut, he stormed into another room. I wasn't sure what to say, so I didn't say anything. But after this happened for several nights in a row, I couldn't resist.

"Dwight," I said, "if that book makes you so mad, why do you keep on reading it?" "Well, I need to read it," he said. It turned out that the book was "Counsels on Diet and Foods" by E. G. White. And there were some things in that book that Dwight had never heard before. But he wasn't so angry about what he was reading. It was the fact that he had been in church all those years and no one had ever shared this book with him before.

"This book could have saved me a lot of trouble," Dwight told me. I can't believe that this was written over a hundred years ago and the very things it says are happening right now in the present. All these other health books are living proof. This has nothing to do with so called religion, this has everything to do with God's love for us." He felt that if he had learned control of appetite earlier in life, he wouldn't have had such a struggle with alcohol.

As Dwight read more of these books, I started to read too. And little by little, we started to put into practice what we had read. We cut down on sugar, quit using dairy products altogether and generally switched to a much more healthful diet.

As Deb and I were making changes in our life, it dawned on me that I was serving a God who truly loves me. I said to Deb, "If these books say you should be healthy then so should the Bible. I started to search the scriptures and found that Christ gave me an owner's manual for my body. God wants me to have a happy and peaceful lifestyle, and to take care of my body so I can be in the very best condition, mentally and spiritually, to serve Him.

As I continued to read my Bible, God impressed me that what we eat has all kinds of consequences on our physical, mental and spiritual state. We can't have a good spiritual state if we're in a lousy mental state, and we can't be in a good mental state if we're in a lousy physical state. In other words, a healthy body and a healthy mind must go hand in hand. More than that, a healthy body is a prelude to a healthy mind.

I read many texts on health in my Bible—including the one that says that whatever I did, whether eating or drinking, should be to the glory of God. And I wanted to do what was right.

I didn't stop there. I drank a lot of soda pop, until I found out how much sugar there was in it. I also drank between 15 to 20 cups of coffee a day. I was so used to caffeine, I could drink 4 cups of coffee at night just before I went to bed and go right to sleep. God sure made some wonderful bodies. There is no way I could abuse an automobile nearly that much and still keep it running! Isn't it strange that we will feed our animals the very best food we can, yet we put all kinds of unhealthy food in our mouths simply because it tastes good, or the TV ads tell us to eat it.

What a battle diet was for us as a family. I found out that besides politics and religion—things you shouldn't talk about—diet was also a sore subject with most people.

Going off dairy was really difficult for me, because I had always loved to cook and knew how to make a lot of good vegetarian dishes. Many of these used eggs, cheese, and/or milk, of course. So when we decided to go off dairy, I felt like I had to learn to cook all over again. And there weren't a lot of good recipe books out there then like there are today.

After we made these changes potlucks were especially challenging.

"Does this have cheese, Mommy?"

Eating to Live

"Do you think there are eggs in this casserole?"

"Is there milk in these scalloped potatoes?"

You can just imagine the list of questions the children might ask, and the responses we would receive from church members who didn't approve of our decision anyway. Fortunately, we thought of a "family rule" that made it so much easier when we ate at a potluck or somebody's house. I went first, and avoided those dishes I had questions about. The children followed, watching and taking the same entrees I did. And they were not to ask any questions—at least not then. This "custom" worked very well for our family and made us a lot less conspicuous. The last thing we wanted to do was to make our friends uneasy.

I tried to do special things for the children to make mealtimes a fun time. For example, when we had pizza we would lay out the pizza pans and lots of topping choices, and everybody had to make their own dough and pizza. It was a lot of fun.

I firmly believe that we should be able to enjoy what we eat. I wanted to give our family good alternatives. Dwight and I wanted to replace the not-so-good things we took away with good things. We did not want our children to grow up rebellious. You have to make it fun and interesting for the kids.

Whenever a person or family makes these kinds of changes, well-meaning friends often brand them as a "legalists." A lot of Christians say you can't work your way into heaven, and this is true. But God gave His best for us. He gave us His Son. And doesn't it make sense that if we are to serve Him, we should give our best to Him? That's what Deb and I decided, and that's really all we were trying to accomplish with our lifestyle changes.

"Why should we settle for mediocrity?" we thought. And although many people didn't understand what we were doing or why we were doing it, our choices had nothing to do with working our way into heaven. Instead, they had everything to do with honoring our Lord and not being a rebuke to Him after what He gave to us.

Although good things were happening, life still had its challenges, of course. I still had my temper and personal problems at the home and office. But for the first time in a long time I had peace in my life. My conscience was clear because I knew I was following God to the best of my ability. I was not holding anything back from my precious Savior. And although my trials didn't go away, I had a foundation (the Bible) to go by as I met them. But I still had no clue this was the beginning of walking with God.

As you can imagine, the devil was less than thrilled with our major turnaround. And he was hard at work, trying to undermine my Christian experience with some of his age-old strategies. If he couldn't keep me from being a Christian at all, he would try to get me to be "too much" of a Christian. In addition, he had a couple of major trials to throw our way.

Gems of Thought

To surrender all our known choices no matter what, not making any excuses for our inefficiencies or weaknesses, and finally to let Christ be all in all—this is our need. I was allowing Him to be my Personal Savior and Friend.

21

Seth

Running Trailmaster's operation in Tulsa continued to be somewhat challenging. My family still worked with us on the business, and we got tired of hauling parts between Michigan and Oklahoma. The idea of having the business all under one roof again became more and more attractive. In addition, employee turnover in Tulsa continued to be high. While Deb's presence in the office really helped me out, Alysha and Natysha needed her at home. That is why after three years in Oklahoma, we decided to move both Trailmaster's manufacturing operation and ourselves back to Michigan.

While in Tulsa, we had recommitted our lives to God. When we moved back to Michigan, some things happened in our lives that made us rely on Jesus even more fully.

Shortly after we moved back to Michigan, we ran into one of the major challenges of our life. It all started the day our son Seth came into the world.

The nurse had just handed Seth to me, and I held him for the very first time. But as I looked down into his sweet little face, I realized he was turning blue.

"Something's wrong with the baby," I said to one of the nurses.

"Oh my," she said, and gave him a little oxygen. He

pinked up right away, so she gave him back.

"Something's wrong with my baby." It took me a couple of seconds to get the nurses attention the second time. Seth was turning blue again!

"Oh my!" The nurse gave Seth another few seconds of oxygen. Once again he pinked right up, and once again she turned away.

"Excuse me!" I was feeling a little frantic. "Something is wrong with my baby!"

Seeing Seth's bluish face, the nurses quickly started oxygen again, and then gathered around, discussing what could be wrong. Soon they sent for another nurse, who gave Seth a quick examination.

"Cleft palate," she announced.

I didn't have a clue what it meant, which, at that moment, was probably a good thing. In any case, Seth's cleft palate was inside, which was why it wasn't noticed right away. His mouth had a hole, and when his tongue covered that hole, it cut off his breath—a very serious condition.

Seth couldn't control his swallowing muscles, and his tongue kept getting up in that hole. So our darling baby lived the first eight weeks of his life in Intensive Care inside a glass case. It was very touch-and-go.

This was extremely hard on both of us. The hospital was 60 miles from where we lived, so we were constantly running back and forth. I was trying to care for Alysha (five years old) and Natysha (just over a year old at the time) while still spending lots of time with Seth. As you can imagine, it all proved to be rather difficult.

Seth looked so small and sick, and they had this big tube down his throat. It really looked to me like he was in pain, which was so very hard to watch. In addition, we had this constant worry that he would die—which he could have done at any time.

Seth

"Don't call me, I'll call you," I told my mother and sister. Fear gripped me every time the phone rang. In fact, I could hardly bear to hear it because I thought the hospital would call with bad news.

Because of the cleft palate, the nurses fed Seth with a feeding tube. It was hard to get enough food into him that way, so the doctors asked if they could put a feeding tube in his side. This would be a surgical procedure, and they also wanted to close his epiglottis at the same time to keep food from coming back up to choke him.

Now, we are not doctors, but we learned that the epiglottis is the little flap that keeps food in your stomach when you stand on your head or go upside down in some other way. This is good, but what if you have food poisoning or a bad case of the flu and need to throw up?

We asked the doctor this question, and he said, "No, Seth will never be able to throw up after the surgery." Now, this might seem like a good thing when you are in the throes of a gut-wrenching stomach flu, but your body has a mechanism to get the poison out, and if it's not allowed to do that, it can also be dangerous. We just weren't comfortable.

Our decision about the surgery really came down to the wire. They had Seth all prepped and ready, and we were drilling the doctor with all of our questions. It was 10:00 in the morning, with surgery scheduled for 11:00—an hour away. We asked the doctor to hold off for a few minutes while Dwight and I went to the chapel to pray. Then we really cried before the Lord.

"We don't want a tube in our baby's side," we told Him. And we begged Him to show us if there was any other way to solve these problems.

When we came out of the chapel, we were both convinced that God would take care of Seth. Our minds were also made up about the proposed surgery: it was not to be done. So we canceled the surgery, and began to look for other options. The doctors at that hospital were not too happy with us.

During this time, I kept suggesting to the doctors that they might make a little plate to cover the hole in Seth's mouth. If there was a plate covering the hole, I reasoned, Seth could move his tongue to the top of his mouth without cutting off his air. Also, with the plate you would not have to worry about him throwing up because that plate would cover the hole in the roof of his mouth.

"No way," the doctors responded. But they did suggest sewing down Seth's tongue. They said they had done that procedure before, although if Seth had a strong tongue, it could rip and go up, cutting off his air anyway. We wanted to do whatever we could to help our baby, but the very idea of a sewed down or ripped tongue was too much for us. We rejected that option as well, and once again the doctors were not happy.

To make matters even worse, when Seth was about 6 weeks old his carbon dioxide levels became too high.

"We need to get these levels down," the doctors informed us, "or your baby will suffer permanent brain damage."

Now we were all for lowering Seth's carbon dioxide levels. But the doctors wanted to accomplish that goal by doing a tracheotomy (a surgery which makes a hole in the throat), and we just didn't want to do that to Seth. So once again we were on our knees, and once again we said "no" to the doctor's recommendation.

The doctors must have had it with us then, because they moved Seth from Intensive Care to a ward filled with retarded children. I guess they figured this is what Seth would turn out to be, so they might as well put him with the others. That was very hard on me. Every day as I visited Seth, I would walk by retarded children who were one, two, three or even four years old, children who had never left the hospital. It was pretty hard not to look at all these other children and think, "Is this where they think Seth belongs?" and "Will Seth really be like this?"

One day, after Seth had been in the ward with retarded children for about a week, a nurse ran to meet me when I came to visit.

"Has the doctor seen you yet?" she wanted to know.

"No," I replied. "Is something wrong?"

"Well, the doctor needs to see you right away." Within minutes a doctor was by my side, telling me that Seth needed to have a tracheotomy as soon a possible. In fact, he wanted to helicopter Seth to Detroit Mercy Hospital right that very hour.

"If this really has to be done, then that's fine," I told them. "But I need to call my husband first to see what he says." In my mind I still wasn't convinced that a tracheotomy was the answer for Seth.

"There's no time for that, Mrs. Hall," the doctor urged. "We need to fly him out of here right away."

"Well, just let me try to call my husband," I insisted. I could tell from the look on the doctor's face that he wasn't too happy with me, but I really needed to know what Dwight thought about all of this. There was just one problem: Dwight was out of town and I wasn't sure how to reach him. Providentially, I was able to reach first his secretary and then Dwight, who just happened to be right by a phone.

"Go ahead," Dwight told me. "Tell them to fly Seth to Detroit Mercy."

"OK," I agreed. "But I want to go with him."

"No," Dwight said. "You stay with the girls. We'll go visit Seth tomorrow."

"But I want to go with him," I wailed. I couldn't bear the thought of them flying my baby off to some unknown hospital in that big helicopter. But in the end, that's what they did. I stood out by the launching pad and watched Seth go, and it took everything I had plus God's strength to keep my feet glued to the ground.

The next day, while Dwight was home for lunch, we got a phone call from the hospital. This naturally gave me a case of the jitters, since every time the phone rang, especially with a doctor on the other end of the line, I just thought "this is the end for Seth."

On this particular day it was a foreign doctor from Detroit Mercy, and try as I might, I simply could not understand what she was saying on the phone. So I finally handed the phone to Dwight.

I still didn't know what the doctor had been saying. But it was plain to see that Dwight was getting all excited about something, and I was pretty dismayed about it all. "Praise the Lord!" Dwight was saying. And then "Great! Go ahead and do it." And then he was praising the Lord again, and saying, "Go ahead! Go ahead!"

By that time I was getting really frustrated. Here my baby is in the hospital about to have a tracheotomy, and he's praising the Lord?

"We're not praising the Lord for anything right now," I fumed, while Dwight was still in the middle of the conversation. "And we're not going to 'go right ahead' and do something when I don't even know what is going on!"

Of course, when Dwight got off the phone he explained it all to me, and we really did have something to praise God over. For one thing, the doctors at Detroit Mercy didn't think Seth needed a tracheotomy. They had been giving him oxygen and his brain was saying, "No need to breathe out. I am getting all this free oxygen." So because of this, the carbon dioxide levels were building up. By taking him off the oxygen little by little, his carbon dioxide levels returned to normal. Isn't it amazing how one little thing can affect our whole system? We are so fearfully and wonderfully made. They also suggested a different type of surgery to install a small plate over the hole in Seth's mouth. Interestingly enough, it was the same idea Dwight had tried to suggest to the doctors in Kalamazoo, but to no avail.

The operation was successful, which was really a miracle. We were extremely thankful, although unbeknownst to us, the longest leg of the "marathon" was yet to begin.

Dwight was away on business when the hospital called at noon one day.

"Seth is ready to come home," I heard a voice say at the other end of the line. Under normal circumstances, this would have been a truly joyous occasion. But after all we had been through, all I could do at that moment was burst into tears. Once again I didn't know exactly where Dwight was, and once again, I needed his support. Fortunately, or should I say, providentially, Dwight called me shortly after the hospital hung up.

"Why are you calling me in the middle of the day?" I asked Dwight. "You never call me in the middle of the day when you're away on business."

"I don't know why I called you now," Dwight replied. "I just felt impressed." After I told Dwight the good news, he told me to go and get Seth.

"But I've never brought a baby home from the hospital by myself before," I burst into tears all over again.

"Well, get your mother to go with you," Dwight tried to encourage me, but he couldn't be there. So I called Mother, and she consented without any second thoughts.

Learning to Walk With God

Now, Seth had lost his sucking and swallowing instincts during his two months of hospitalization and tube feeding. I had to learn how to feed Seth through a tube before I could even take him home. My mother wanted to learn how also. In fact, God used her to keep reassuring me that everything would be OK all the way to the hospital. When we finally arrived, I did learn how to tube feed Seth. My mother, on the other hand, just froze. She simply couldn't do it. There was another part for her to play, however. Seth's "plate", or "dentures" as we called them, had to be cleaned in a special way each day. I just couldn't seem to do that, but my mother could. So I was the only one who fed Seth for all those months, but my mother came over to clean his "dentures" every day. Dwight and all the rest of the family loved him. So raising Seth truly was a team effort!

When Seth came home, he still had to be hooked up to a monitor. That thing was always going off. Sometimes it would go off just because his breaths were short. So we would rush into Seth's room at all hours of the day and night. He was OK, but we were really stressed.

Maybe it was because Seth had been in the hospital for so long, or because we were so afraid that he was going to die, but Dwight really struggled to bond with his son. For a long time he wouldn't even hold Seth. He just put his hand on him, and prayed.

"Dwight, you need to hold him," I would chide gently. I could tell he struggled with the thought.

I determined to slowly teach Seth to swallow again. So I cut a hole in the nipple of a bottle, and would let a little bit of formula run down his throat. It took five long months, but when Seth turned 7 months old, his itty bitty fingers finally grasped the 4 oz. bottle. The wires hooking Seth to his monitor were truly formidable.

Seth

Many mornings when Dwight woke early he would go in and untangle Seth from the wires.

"Those wires are going to kill the baby," he would tell me. One morning I got up before Dwight and went in to look at Seth. I couldn't believe how tangled up he was, and went to tell Dwight about it.

"Those wires are going to kill the baby," I said, repeating his previous thoughts.

"I know," Dwight replied. "That's what I've been telling you every morning." We were afraid to take Seth off the monitor and even more afraid not to, but in the end, we took him off.

Seth was sick an awful lot that first year. In fact, it was hard to get and keep enough food down him. When he reached his first birthday, he weighed only about 10 pounds.

The people at church didn't seem to understand what I was going through. Some of them felt I was doting over him too much, because they saw me feeding him every 2-3 hours. They told me so, too, and some of their comments really hurt. On more than one occasion I went into the church bathroom to have myself a good cry.

When Seth was 14 months old, he had the first of two surgeries to correct the problem. Before the surgery, the doctor told me he would be grafting some skin over the hole in Seth's mouth.

And I thought, "You know, I've really done a lot here. I've tube fed Seth for so many months, and Dwight's never even learned. The least Dwight can do is give some of his skin. So if Seth needs some skin, they can take it off of him."

For some reason I worried a lot about "who" would give Seth skin, but my fears were laid to rest when I finally asked the doctor. Nobody would have to give skin—they would use Seth's own!

Although teaching Seth to drink from a bottle was a major accomplishment, teaching him how to chew and eat food was even more of a challenge. Seth was two years old when he finally started to eat any solid foods.

What we went through with Seth was tough, really tough. But it was an important part of our spiritual journey. It made us turn to God in a way we had never done before. It also drew us closer together as a couple, and for that I will always be thankful.

Gems of Thought

As painful as this experience was, it did have a major, positive effect. It drove us to our knees, closer together, and closer to God. Day by day we didn't know if Seth would live or die, so we had to put him in God's hands. Sometimes I felt that this had happened because of my past sins, and I really searched my soul. We don't believe that now, but it is easy to think those kinds of thoughts when you're in such a stressful situation.

22

Finding My Niche

When we moved back to Coldwater, I became very involved in church activities. Having given my heart to God, I wanted to serve Him in any way possible. To do all for Jesus that I possibly could. Before very long I was given my opportunity. First I became a lesson study teacher, then an elder. Then, less than a year later, I was asked to be the head elder.

As if that wasn't enough, I served on the church board and the school board, this in addition to giving Bible studies in the evening. I was indeed a "very busy" Christian.

Of course, during this whole time I still had our successful business. I traveled all over the world, kept incredibly busy, and thought I was living God's plan for my life. When I went on business trips, I saw people all over the world who were hurting. I wanted to share Christ, and I wanted to work full-time for God.

As I drew closer to Jesus, my secular business became less important to me. In time, I even began to pray for a way out of it. In fact, I prayed for God's leading in my career for four full years—morning and evening—before I discovered the job God wanted me to do.

At one point I had been approached about being a youth pastor. I liked the idea. In fact, I got real excited. I thought God was going to let me work with the youth. Because of the problems

I had experienced, I thought this an answer to prayer. However, the doors closed.

"Lord," I prayed. "I have come to know truth, and I love it. This seems like the perfect fit. Why have the doors shut?" Even though I questioned, in the recesses of my heart, I knew God had something for me.

Since I had, and still have, a Type A personality, I wanted to do something NOW! All I could think of was working for the Lord. Yet our business kept growing and becoming more and more profitable. During those four years, I kept thinking the Lord is coming soon. There are millions to be warned and Lord, I know I am not the best, but I am a willing servant. Little did I realize God had a work for me to do. I just needed more training. God wanted me to begin a study in a subject I still have not mastered. This class is called Faith 101.

A few years later, a speaker came to our Michigan church. He spoke about how most of us are asleep, coming to church thinking we are OK, but deep down we are wanting. We had him over to our house for dinner, and he started asking me some very pointed questions. After a short time, he said, "Dwight. The Lord has blessed you very much, and I see you have a great burden for souls. These books you keep talking about (*Patriarchs and Prophets*, *Prophets and Kings*, *The Desire of Ages*, *The Acts of the Apostles*, and *The Great Controversy*—The *Bible Study Companion Set*) have changed your life. Reading them with your Bible has not only opened your eyes, but from what you have told me, they have made you a different person. If they have made such a change in your life, maybe God would have you market these books to the world. The Lord has given you marketing abilities. You understand distribution methods. You should ask the Lord about this."

When he got done saying this, I actually heard an audible voice in my head, not just an impression. I had never experienced that before. Just as clearly as someone talking to me it said, "Dwight, this is what I want you to do!" There was no mistake. I must have looked awfully strange because the speaker asked, "What do you think?" But the way he looked at me made me recompose myself enough to answer, "It sounds good. I will pray about it and let you know in a week."

For the next seven days, I could not think of anything else. I knew God had spoken. It seemed so clear that there really was no mistaking it. God continued to impress upon my mind, "Get the books out." No more audible voice; just that still, small voice. And the more I prayed, the more strongly I felt convicted that selling the *Bible Study Companion Set* was exactly what God wanted me to do.

I accepted. What a huge burden lifted off my chest. God had waited for the perfect time.

I asked Bill if he would be willing to sell books instead of suspension systems, and he agreed. As mentioned in an earlier chapter, Bill had become a committed Christian at the same time I had, and had become very knowledgeable about the Bible. We prayed about the name of this ministry, and, with the help of my brother Dan, came up with the name Remnant Publications.

While my father, Uncle Rudy, and brothers Rudy and Dan all went together with me to buy the first 300,000 books, my brother Dan and I did most of the work. And while we didn't know much about the book business at that point, we did know that God would be our helper. That He wanted us to do this, and because of His leading, it would work.

In the beginning, we sold the five *Bible Study Companion* books one volume at a time. But we soon began selling them as a set, which we called the *Bible Study Companion Set*. During this time, our family still owned and operated Trailmaster. But as the book business grew I began praying about my other business. Trailmaster was making good money, but I wanted to devote my life full time to God's work.

As you may know, it's not that easy to sell a specialized business like Trailmaster. You have to find the right kind of buyer with the right amount of money, and even then it takes time. In addition, many buyers want the prior owner to stay on and run the business indefinitely. But while I was willing to help with the transition for awhile, I definitely wanted out of the business.

At one point I worked with a potential buyer for a whole year, only to have the deal fall through the day before it was final. And that was a big letdown for me.

"Lord," I prayed, "if you want me to devote more time to selling these books, please send the right buyer for Trailmaster.

The second time a buyer backed out on me, I decided to call and see why he was hesitating. He agreed to meet and talk about it, so we did. And in the end, he decided to buy the business. That was a very happy day for me, but it certainly wasn't the end of my involvement in the company.

I stayed on for a year to help with the transition, and during that year I worked harder than ever. Because we had sold the company, family members began to leave for other employment. As for myself, the fact that I had sold the company made me feel more pressured than ever to make it a success. In the year following the sale, I worked more hours than ever before. And all this was in addition to starting my bookselling ministry, and my many church-related responsibilities.

Gems of Thought

God has a work for each one of us to do. No matter what our education or background. Remember the demoniac in Luke 8:26-40. When Christ touched his heart, he went into the city and when Jesus came back, the town came to listen. The bottom line is we need to have an experience with Him. After that, it is not preaching; it is sharing those experiences. Friends, we must never despair. As we continue to draw closer and trust in Him, He will take care of us.

Finally graduation with my Cobra.

Training to be special
Airborne Rangers.

Answer to second part of my
prayer, getting married.

Alysha next to my Jeep.

113

The American Dream?

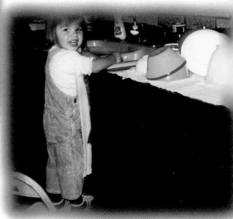

Starting them young, Alysha
helping with kitchen duties.

Seth our miracle baby.

Alysha, Natysha and Seth.

Learning to spend time with family.

Natysha doing her part.

Moving to the wilderness,
our front yard view.

Starting our house, Seth
helping out.

Our home, the place for character building.

Building faith with our backyard bear.

School with Alysha.

Cleaning our deck, one of Seth's duties.

A lesson in slowing down.

Building character in the snow five foot on the level.

An exciting time getting the mail twice a week.

Our children learning the "just because" principle.

The art of canning,
Natysha learning by example.

Seth making peanut butter.

Alysha canning, learning to do things
thoroughly promptly and well.

Learning to take time with a
simple walk.

A good way to learn patience.

Watching the wildlife, a black wolf.

Seth learning to chop down his first tree.

Allowing God to teach and speak to us in nature.

My father Darwin and my two brothers
Dan and Rudy.

Growing as a family.

No longer afraid of the bear.

Printing operation, Remnant Publications.

23

My Life as a Pharisee

As I continued to study my Bible and make changes in my life, I did not really notice others around me and see that they weren't living up to what I had learned. So enthralled was I about my lessons that I had no time to look at the faults of others. These new truths were like fresh air, and the Lord truly was my first love. I made the changes because I wanted to, I knew it was the right thing to do, and because I knew the Lord only wanted the best for me. Like the Bible says in the first part of Psalms 40:8, "I delight to do thy will, O my God." It truly was a love relationship.

The Bible became more and more real to me as I kept studying it, and I enjoyed sharing what I read. Because of my excitement, I just assumed when I told my friends they would be excited, too. To my disappointment they would say, "Be careful Dwight. You don't want to get too excited about these things." And "I think your growth in Christ is good, but remember not to get unbalanced." I would think, Well, I have only just become a Christian. They have been at it so much longer, so maybe I am reading this wrong. So I would go back and read again, and become even more convicted. I began to realize my friends did not really want to know. They were comfortable the way they were.

My Type A personality told me to prove it by the Word of God to them. I honestly thought that if I could show them from

Scripture, they would change. Boy, was I in for a big surprise. Little then did I know the old saying, "A man convinced against his will is of the same opinion still."

Why is it people defend wrong so much so that any unbiased person with only a little common sense can see it? I just wanted to be right. IF I was wrong, I wanted to change it like NOW! Too many of us have grown up a certain way and just accept many things as truth.

Over time, something happened to me so imperceptibly I did not even see it. Little by little, I began to take my eyes off of Christ and started looking at others to see what they were doing or where they should be. I let these faults of others become my all-consuming interest. Looking back, I recognized my old nemesis, hypocrisy, rearing its ugly head.

During this time I read Malachi 3:10, where God says "Bring ye all the tithes into the storehouse, that there may be meat in mine house, and prove me now herewith, saith the Lord of hosts, if I will not open you the windows of heaven, and pour you out a blessing, that there shall not be room enough to receive it".

As I read this verse, I wondered what God meant by bringing in "all" the tithes. Was He talking about money only? Or was He talking about the talent of time as well.

I started thinking about the talent of time. Everybody has it. Since God asks us to give our tithe before we do anything else, I decided to give Him the first part of every day. I also read about the Children of Israel and how they got their manna—the "Bread of Life"—every morning. This strengthened my resolve to give God the first part of my day.

But when I studied, I studied to prove someone wrong. I have to say I did it honestly. I did not do this to be mean. I had such a burden for souls, and I truly thought I was approaching this from the right direction.

But while watching the faults of others and giving God the first part of every day, I did not realize I neglected my own family. That there were things I should have done that I wasn't doing.

My Life as a Pharisee

During this time I saw some of the same things Dwight did, although I didn't say much about it. I knew Dwight could see the faults in other people but not in us, but he was my spiritual leader and I thought he would figure it out sooner or later.

Myself, I didn't like to say much about other people. I knew I had faults myself, so I didn't see how I could pick out theirs. And if I ever did slip and say something about someone, Dwight would remind me in a hurry.

"Well, what about yourself?" he would say. "What are you doing that you shouldn't be doing?"

When we first got married I would talk right back to Dwight, but I soon learned that I could never out-talk him. I also found that being quiet was the best way to really get under his skin. Of course, as I grew in Christ, more and more of the time I was quiet for the right reasons.

During this time in our lives, Sabbath mornings were especially difficult for me. As a mother, I found it easy to be organized with only one child. But when we had three, I lost it.

On a typical Sabbath morning, I made breakfast, dressed the kids, got food ready for the potluck and made sure everything we needed for the day was in the van. Even then, I always missed something. It could be socks, or shoes, or a hairbow. I could not find it.

During all this time my husband (Mr. Scholar—as I called him then) would be tucked away in the den, studying. Dwight never likes to be late. So at the appropriate time he would emerge from the den, all dressed and ready for church, sit in the van and blow the horn.

By this time, I was wrung wet from the morning's whirl of activities. With not much time to get myself ready, I would quickly slip something on and brush my hair while flying on the way to church.

Learning to Walk With God

"Why can't you be on time, Deb?" Dwight would always ask as I huffed into the front seat of the car. But since I couldn't think of anything good to say to him at that moment, I didn't usually say anything.

Anyway, I had to organize my thoughts before I got to church, since I was usually leading out in either the kindergarten or cradle roll division. Then of course I was supposed to put on a smile, go upstairs, and keep the children quiet during the service while Dwight sat up on the platform.

Dwight kept telling me that if I would just get organized, things would go much more smoothly. But for quite some time, irritation prevented me from listening to him.

God was teaching me a lesson so many of us need to learn, simply put, "Don't throw the baby out with the bath water." Even though Dwight was critical in areas, there were things he said that were absolutely true. Self raises its ugly head, but so often we have our ugly head glasses on so we just don't see it. God was helping me to take these glasses off so I could look at me and pray earnestly for my areas with Christ.

During this time, I studied my Bible for about an hour and a half every morning before family worship, and really enjoyed the blessing I received. I had read in Exodus 16 about the manna, how the Israelites were to gather it each morning, every one "according to each one's need" (verse 16). I understood the manna to stand for the "bread" of an experience with Jesus, for Jesus said, "I am the bread of life" (John 6:48). So I made a commitment to study God's word without fail every morning, before the "dew" (or busy-ness of the day) melted away that opportunity for good.

But while I understood those important Biblical truths, I skipped over some other parts of the story that are equally important. As I just mentioned, every one was to gather according to his need. When a person gathered too much for themselves that day, the manna "bred worms and stank." In other words, we need to study according to our need and apply it to our lives. But if we start gathering extra—talking but not walking the walk—that stinks! Of course I didn't realize it then, but that very thing was happening in my life. And as you might imagine, it wasn't well received by some of my fellow church members. In fact, people at church were beginning to say some disturbing things about me. Some of them even called me a Pharisee.

For someone who had vowed never to be a hypocrite, being called a Pharisee is quite a serious allegation. At the time it didn't bother me, however, because I just thought they were wrong. It took an upsetting experience with my family to finally open my eyes and show me who was really in the wrong. . .

Gems of Thought

Truth can come in a variety of packages, and most of the time the package isn't wrapped in beautiful Christmas, birthday, or gift paper. It could be wrapped in garbage bags. Many times you actually have to dig in the trash to find truth. All of us must learn to go to the truth Giver and ask what is truth, then search unbiased to do that which is good.

24

Coming to Grips
With Myself

One Wednesday morning quiet time found me studying for my prayer meeting talk for that evening. According to my custom at that time, I was studying for everyone else but me. Once again, my eyes were off of Jesus and focused on other people. I felt I had something very important to share that night, and hoped everyone would attend.

"I'll be home for lunch today," I told Deb as I headed out the door for work.

"Oh, right you will," she retorted, rolling her eyes. Deb had good reason to believe I wouldn't come home for lunch, because I hardly ever did. I was usually too busy, but on this day I really did plan to make it home. To tell you the truth, Deb's answer to my promise made me kind of mad.

"I will be home today." She didn't answer. She just rolled her eyes again. "I'll prove you wrong," I snapped, heading out the door. "And I WILL be home for lunch today."

When Dwight said he'd be home for lunch that day, I guess I was pretty sarcastic with him.

"Don't tell me what you're going to do, if you're not going to do it!" I felt like shouting at his retreating figure. And I knew he wouldn't be home for lunch, because he never was.

126

Coming to Grips With Myself

That morning, things went very well at work. It was close to noon and I was just ready to leave for lunch when my secretary called to say that a business associate had stopped by to see me.

"They've traveled a long way, Dwight", she said, "even though they don't have an appointment."

"Can they wait until after lunch?" I asked.

"No. They have to be on their way."

The minute I started talking to that person, I knew I would never make it home for lunch. And I was ticked.

"How could this have happened to me," I wondered. "And what will Deb say now?"

I didn't have to wait long to find out, because I decided to give her a call.

"Hi, Deb," I said.

"I know," she replied. "You're not coming home for lunch."

"That's right." Being a short-tempered person myself, I was almost angry that she didn't yell at me. But that wasn't her manner.

"You don't understand," I tried. "Let me explain."

"I really don't care. You always have an excuse. I like it better when you say I don't understand because at least you're right there," she replied calmly.

"I will be home before prayer meeting," I concluded. "So would you please lay out my clothes and Bible for me so I can change quickly? That way, we can get there on time."

"OK, Dwight." Her sugar sweet tone almost irritated me.

Of course, I wasn't a bit surprised when Dwight called. I knew he meant well, but a lot of times he said he would do things and then didn't get them done. And he put a lot more effort out for others than he did for me.

At the end of the day and just as I was leaving the office, something else came up. I quickly realized that I wouldn't even have time to go home before prayer meeting. Once again, I was

127

on the phone to my wife. And before I could even tell her what I wanted, she surprised me by saying "I know, Dwight. You want me to get the kids around and bring your clothes to you at work so we can leave from there." I was shocked that she knew me so well! Why is it that certain problems each of us have tend to constantly follow us around?

When my family did arrive at the office, I was still busy working. Deb started to tell me about her day, but it was obvious I wasn't listening. Her voice trailed off into quietness, but I hardly even noticed. Unfortunately for him, my son Seth wasn't quite as perceptive:

"Dad, guess what I did today?" I was too busy to answer and knew that I wouldn't get my work done if I got involved in a conversation, so I ignored him. So he tried again. "Hey, Dad, guess what I did today?"

Seeing he wasn't going to give me any peace unless I answered, I looked up from my work.

"Seth, can't you see that I'm trying to write? I'm busy. Talk to me later—after prayer meeting," I ordered. "Not now."

By this time, it was 7:15—only 15 minutes before prayer meeting would begin.

"Dwight, don't you think you should get ready to leave now?" This time it was Deb who broke into my thoughts.

Without a moment's hesitation I snapped back, "Don't you think I can tell time?" Once again, Deb was quiet. 5 minutes passed by, and finally I was ready to get dressed for prayer meeting.

"Get the kids in the car and strapped in their seats so I don't have to wait," I instructed Deb. Then I hurriedly began to fling off my clothes and dress in the clean outfit she had prepared and brought for me. Soon I had everything on but my belt. Deb had forgotten my belt! I was furious. Couldn't she remember this one little thing? What had she done all day, anyway?

"How could you have forgotten my belt?" I exploded at Deb when I got into the car. I slammed the door and squealed out of the parking lot, venting my anger in a torrent of words as I went.

Coming to Grips With Myself

Although Dwight really blew up that night, we went through this scenario on so many occasions. Get yourself ready. Get everything else ready. And by all means, have the kids ready and in the car. Why? So that he didn't have to wait.

"How could you have forgotten my belt!" Dwight was driving furiously and talking just as fast.

"You know, shoes, socks, pants, shirt, belt! There are only so many things you have to remember!" Dwight ranted on and on.

"Here you go again," I thought to myself as our car raced toward the church. "Ranting and raving on the way to church. You're really losing it, Dwight." But I didn't say a thing.

In my mind, I always rationalized Dwight's behavior. Either he was stressed out because of his work, or feeling very frustrated, or whatever. Other families had their troubles, too, and we would just have to put up with it.

Deb finally did break her code of silence, after I stopped yelling. But when she did speak, it was only to remind me that I was driving at a rather high rate of speed. And my response was typical for the day.

"Don't you think I know how to drive?" I blasted back. "I know how fast I'm going, and you don't have to tell me!"

In the back seat, Natysha hadn't caught on to my mood.

"Dad, guess what I did today?"

"Be quiet," I snapped. "I'm trying to figure out what to say to these people at prayer meeting tonight. They really need to hear the truth about getting ready for Jesus to come.

Believe it or not, we actually pulled, or shall I say skidded, into the church at 7:28! Because I can't stand to be late, I pasted on my happy smile, leaped out of the truck and literally ran into the church. Then I shook hands with everybody.

"Welcome to prayer meeting," I said. "You won't be sorry you came, because you're going to hear something very important tonight."

That night I stood in front of those people and told them that very soon, probation would close. Worse yet, they wouldn't even know when it happened. So I tried to impress them with the shortness of life. Some of them might even have heart attacks or accidents on the way home. Were they ready for Jesus to come? I was very serious.

The people didn't say much as they left that night. For once, it was quiet in our vehicle too. I looked at Deb and said, "These people don't understand that if they don't change their lives they will be lost!"

At that very instant, I heard a voice in my head. It was that still small voice, and it said, "Dwight, if you don't change your life, you'll be lost. You are a Pharisee. Worse than that, you are a blind Pharisee." For the first time in a long time, I saw myself for what I really was, and it hit me like a ton of bricks.

Gems of Thought

I had been honest in my desire to be a Christian, and I thought I was doing right. Yet I kept hearing that still small voice saying, "You know much of my word, Dwight. You search the Scriptures, for in them you think you have eternal life. But you will not come to me that you might have life." (paraphrase of John 5:39-40)

25

Searching My Soul

When I got home, I fell on my knees and prayed.

"What is my problem, Lord? I'm trying so hard to be a Christian. Why do I still lose my temper? Where are the victories, Lord?" Most of all I wanted to know, "Why am I a Pharisee?"

That night, the Holy Spirit convicted me that I was the epitome of Matthew 23:24—a "blind guide" that was "straining out a knat" and "swallowing a camel." More than that, I was paying tithe and omitting the weightier matters of the law, like justice, mercy and faith.

God was telling me that I was too proud to give Him my all. That I thought I was better than other people. As I prayed that night, I reminded the Lord that I had stood for the right, that some people in my church were only superficial Christians, that I had suffered much for the cause of Christ—why, I didn't even have time to spend with my family. Because I was constantly working for God, I figured He should be proud of me.

Yet in my heart, I knew others were tired of my preaching. In church, some of them would rather turn and walk away than shake my hand.

As I agonized over these things, God impressed me to read Revelation 2:2-7:

"I know thy works, and thy labour, and thy patience, and

how thou canst not bear them which are evil: and thou hast tried them which say they are apostles, and are not, and hast found them liars: And hast borne, and hast patience, and for my name's sake has laboured, and hast not fainted. Nevertheless I have somewhat against thee, because thou hast left thy first love. Remember therefore from whence thou art fallen, and repent, and do the first works; or else I will come unto thee quickly, and will remove thy candlestick out of his place, except thou repent . . . He that hath an ear, let him hear what the Spirit saith unto the churches; To him that overcometh will I give to eat of the tree of life, which is in the midst of the paradise of God."

It reminded me that I needed to renew my first love, that it did not matter how much knowledge I had—even though knowledge is important. I lacked the everyday experience with Jesus. When I started looking at others instead of Jesus, worrying about their faults instead of my own—that is when I left my first love.

I didn't admit all these things without a struggle. In fact, it was a real fight. I pointed out to God that people were finding salvation because of my work publishing books. But once again the Holy Spirit lead me to a verse. "For what is a man profited, if he shall gain the whole world, and lose his own soul?" (Matthew 16:26).

Then I asked God why I was not winning victories over my "besetting" sins.

"Dwight, you need to take time to be holy," the still small voice answered back.

"But I don't have time to be . . ." I started in, but couldn't even finish my sentence. God impressed me right then and there that I needed to change my priorities—that I was studying the Bible for everyone else, but not for myself. That I was trying to astound the world with what I had found in the Bible, but that it was heart knowledge, not head knowledge, I needed. I needed to make the Scriptures practical. I was honest with what I had been thinking. I wanted so much to be that person that would walk with God. I also wanted to share it with everybody else. It wasn't to tell everybody I was better, but I wanted them to see how they needed to make a change not to keep playing church.

Then He impressed me to read Isaiah 30:15. "For thus saith the Lord God, the Holy One of Israel; in returning and rest shall ye be saved; in quietness and in confidence shall be your strength: and ye would not."

I had read that verse before, but never in this light. In my heart, I knew that I was under too much time pressure at work. Yes, even in my ministry. I did not spend enough time with my family. My home life needed major improvement. While I could see the faults of others clearly, I needed to deal with my own. One minute I could be teaching a Sabbath School class, and the next minute yelling at my wife. In addition, sometimes I disciplined my children out of anger.

Luke 16:10 says, "He that is faithful in that which is least is faithful also in much." But I had been leaving the little things off in my life. I was so busy helping other people, and being important, that I skipped over my own faults.

God showed me that the first work I needed to do was that of self-development. I saw how incredibly important it is to be a real Christian in the little things, so God could trust me with greater things.

I needed to put God first in my life, and realize that His priorities were not the same as my priorities. "Seek ye first the kingdom of God, and His righteousness, and all these things will be added unto you" (Matthew 6:33).

God impressed me to read the story of Nicodemus in the book The Desire of Ages when he came to visit Jesus after dark.

"Are you the Messiah?" Nicodemus wanted to know. But Jesus never answered his question—at least not directly.

"Nicodemus," he said, "you need to be born again. To be fully converted." In other words, even if I convinced you that I was the Messiah, in and of itself this would not save you.

I could relate to Nicodemus. He had been a blind Pharisee like me. Because I didn't have Christ in my heart at all times, I was actually a curse to my family. While I naturally wanted to do great things for God, I had to realize that some of my unimportant things were great in the eyes of God.

When I finally realized this, the Bible once more came alive. That night, when I held a prayer meeting but blew up at my wife and children, became an important step in my spiritual journey. When I focused on Jesus again instead of other people, my peace returned. And this time when I opened the Word of God, I was reading it for me.

Gems of Thought

I wish I could say after that night when I realized my Pharisaac faults so fully that I instantly transformed. Unfortunately, this was not the case. We know from the Bible that Christianity is a growth experience, that sanctification is the work of a lifetime.

26

Choices and Changes

By this time Alysha was attending church school, and, as might be expected, our conservative choices created more than a few lifestyle challenges. One particular incident involved a special lunch where all the children would trade sandwiches. This was a problem for us, because about half of the children had meat in their lunches on a regular basis. We didn't want Alysha to trade the sandwich we sent her for another if we weren't sure what it was.

Then there were the pizza parties, but we didn't eat cheese. And caramel apples, but we didn't eat sugar. Once when one of Alysha's classmates brought in a chocolate birthday cake, Alysha went to the teacher.

"We don't eat chocolate," Alysha said.

"Oh, I know. I don't either." The teacher replied. "But this is a special occasion. It's OK to have a piece."

"Well, Momma wouldn't want me to eat that cake," Alysha said.

"We don't want to hurt any feelings," the teacher whispered, glancing toward the lady who brought the cake. "It really is OK to have a little piece." So Alysha did.

Of course, I wasn't any too happy when Alysha came

home and told me these things. I had worked hard to teach Alysha about the best diet for her body, so it really disturbed me to have someone teach her something else. We ran into a lot of incidents like this. Ultimately, it wasn't a "big thing" that led us to start home-schooling Alysha. It was a combination of "little things." Sometimes it is hard to live the way you believe and still have your friends like and respect you. We just wanted the freedom to do what we believed was right. It was important to us to be able to train our children consistently. To tell them one thing and have others tell them something different—especially teachers—was more than just confusing.

"Let this mind be in you, which was also in Christ Jesus," the Bible says (Philippians 2:5). We understood that having the mind of Jesus, or knowing Jesus more fully, involved keeping our minds clear so He could speak to us. While we knew that dietary choices (for example, not eating a piece of chocolate cake) would not save us, we reasoned that if it wasn't healthy, why eat it? We wanted to follow the counsel of that verse, "Whether therefore ye eat, or drink, or whatsoever ye do, do all to the glory of God" (1 Corinthians 10:31).

Part of the glory of God is to have His character. As Deb and I decided that we wanted to have the mind of Christ, we chose to put into practice the very things and principles that would help us as we moved in that direction.

A lot of people didn't understand why we changed our diet. Although we were careful not to tell others what to do, people seemed to get agitated over our choices anyway.

About this time we were feeling a need to travel a lot more than we were. Dwight was really on fire to get the Bible Study Companion Sets out into the churches, and we needed to be free to do that.

Choices and Changes

We also wanted to spend more time together as a family. In spite of Dwight's ambition to spend more time with us, he was still much too busy. And much of what he was doing was church work. Together, we began to feel a need to quit all our church jobs and take a break. To move away, if necessary, to slow down our lives.

You see, my problem was that if I lost my temper, I would pray that night and agonize with the Lord to forgive me. But the next day, if I came under pressure or my will was crossed, I lost my temper all over again.

I couldn't seem to gain the victories that I needed. I had learned that victory was possible and expected by Christ, and my failures frustrated me. So I prayed to God about it. I wanted to know the problem, and fix it. Specifically, I wanted to know why I wasn't gaining the victories I wanted so badly.

Then God, through His word and the impression of the Holy Spirit, led me to a principle I had never realized before: that if we have too much on our mind, it is difficult to make the needed changes in our lives.

At one time, Trailmaster employed close to 50 people, and one of my jobs was personnel management. I learned some important lessons from the people who came through my office.

Some of our employees would come into my office and say, "Dwight, I have a problem."

"What's the problem?" I would wonder.

"Well, I need a raise," they would reply.

"Why do you need more money?" I would ask.

The answer would invariably be, "Well, I just bought a car," or "I don't have enough money for my house payment this month." In all my years of running that business, no one ever told me "Well, I'm doing so well on my job that I feel I'm worth more than I'm being paid." Not once.

Now here is a question: if I gave those employees more

money, would I have invested well, or would they just go out and get into bigger financial trouble? The truth is that when given more money, many people who have trouble handling their finances just go on to bigger and deeper troubles.

In my own life, I was coming into God's office every morning and every night asking not only for forgiveness, but the victory.

"Lord, I have a problem," I would say

And the still small voice would inquire, "What's the problem, Dwight?"

"Well, I need more grace," I would reply.

"And why do you need more grace?" the query would come back.

The answer would invariably be, "Well, I was under a lot of pressure at work and I lost my temper again," or "Deb crossed my will today, and I really set her straight."

In a way, I acted just like my employees who had trouble managing their finances, only I had trouble with grace. I wanted God to give me more and lots of it, but by placing myself in pressure-packed situations and allowing my mind to be preoccupied with too many things, I wasn't making very good use of the grace He had already given me!

I was too busy running my business and doing everything else to really gain those victories, not doing what I needed to do in order to gain lasting victories. I needed to take time in my life—time to know God's will for me.

It is true that I diligently took time to study my Bible and pray to God. But I never took time to commune with God and find out what He really wanted me to do. Its like someone once told me, most people are so busy just trying to make a living they have no time to make any money. You can do a lot of good things and work very hard, but never get anywhere. As I read more and more of my Bible, I became convicted that a move into the quietness of the country—away from the busy-ness of my life—was exactly what I needed. At that point, we didn't have the vaguest idea where we would go. The Northwest sounded interesting, or maybe even northern Michigan. Of one thing we were sure—we did want to make a change, and as God led, we were going.

Gems of Thought

You send your children to school, tell them they will tell you what you need to know. Then when there are conflicting views, your children get confused. They think this is my Mom and Dad, they know what they are doing. But they sent me to school to learn from the teachers, maybe they know more than my parents. It is so hard on the children.

Deb and I learned that our children needed to be taught God's principles. We let them know that looking to men or women only, no matter how high their office will only confuse the best of minds.

27

As God Leads the Way

One Sabbath while sitting on the platform as an elder, the appearance of some old acquaintances in the back pew surprised me. They were the parents of Tom Waters, one of my roommates and very good friends from academy.

I had not seen or heard from Tom for 13 or 14 years, so I was anxious to hear how he was doing. Wondering whether Tom's parents would remember me, and what they would remember, I hurried up to them after church.

"Hi! I'm Dwight Hall," I said. "You probably don't remember me, I knew your son Tom in academy."

"Oh yes, we remember you," they replied starting to smile.

I'll bet I know why they remember me, I thought. It's that big black cloud following me around again. Tom had also been in some trouble during his academy days. In fact, I had last seen him the summer after I had been kicked out of academy. I had driven over to visit Tom in my sleek black Cobra, and we had ridden around town, doing things we shouldn't have done.

They told me Tom lived in Montana, selling real estate. But they never told me that Tom had changed his life. That he, too, had found his way back to God.

The Waters gave me Tom's phone number. I wanted to call Tom soon—to see how he was, and share with him what God was doing in my life. But while I had good intentions, Tom's number stayed tucked away in my wallet for two or three months. When I finally did call Tom, I was surprised at the things we had in common. Tom had also married, had become the father of two girls and a son, and had come back to God. I truly enjoyed hearing about the changes in Tom's life, and sharing my own experience with him.

During the course of our conversation, Tom mentioned that I would be welcome to come and visit sometime if I was ever out that way. In God's providence I had planned a business trip to California in just a few weeks.

"I might be able to change my plane tickets so I could stop by on the way home," I told him. I'll never forget Tom's response to my suggestion, because it really shocked me.

"My wife and I will pray about that," he replied, promising to call me back shortly.

Pray about that? I wondered to myself as the phone clicked. What's the big deal? Didn't he just invite me? Then what does he need to pray about?

Tom did call me back in a couple of hours, and we made the final arrangements for my trip. In addition, Tom offered to send me some tapes about wilderness living.

"That's fine," I told him. When the tapes arrived, I did listen to them. They moved me and touched me, because Tom and his wife Alane had already done many of the very things God was showing me. It hit me hard.

This is from the Lord, I thought. Here was a friend—someone I even knew—doing some of the very things God impressed me to do. I didn't tell Deb about all this—not yet. But I became very anxious to see Tom, Alane, and their family. I wondered if they were living the way they talked on those tapes, if their children were obedient, and if they had a well ordered home.

I am thankful to say that visiting the Waters did not disappoint me. Not that they were perfect, nor that I expected them to be. But their home did reflect their Christianity. In the few days I visited, I could plainly see that Tom and his wife were actually applying the principles they talked about on those tapes.

When I first called Tom, neither of us had mentioned the spiritual changes taking place in our lives. All that changed when I got to his home. Tom and his family showed in everything they did that they had experienced a very real and personal turnaround.

While in Tom's home, I watched each person rather closely. I could see they were really striving to do God's will. Allison, Emily, and Josiah especially impressed me.

Now, my own children were very obedient; that's the way they were raised. If I said, "Don't do this," they didn't do it. They didn't ask twice, either, because they knew what would happen if they did. But in my heart I knew that when I spoke to my children, it tended to be with irritation or because I was upset. I did not have the right attitude. And there were times my children obeyed out of fear.

But I saw something different in the Waters' family. Tom and Alane truly did spend time with their children, and with very positive results.

I talked to Tom about it, and he told me that he, too, had once been too busy. But God in His mercy had spoken to Tom's heart and impressed him to change.

"The most important thing in my life now is Jesus, my wife, and my children," Tom told me. "I want to spend time with my children, and raise them to be like Jesus."

Before I left, Tom and Alane invited me to bring my family for a visit. I was happy for the invitation, and could hardly wait to share their tapes with Deb. It occured to me, however, that Deb might not want to listen to the tapes. So I came up with the idea of a little vacation.

"Why don't we go camping up north for the weekend?" I asked Deb. We had a nice motor home at the time, and our church owned a nice rustic campground on the shores of Lake Au Sable. Convincing Deb to take a vacation wasn't too hard: after all, she had wanted one of those for years.

When we got up north, I parked and got everything in order. I kept praying that God would give me the right time to share the tapes. I wanted the kids in bed and complete silence where she could listen without any distractions. I think back now as to why I wanted her to listen. I had already been thinking about moving out west. I knew that she would not have a problem with the tapes. I prayed it would go deeper than that. I made a campfire while Deb put Alysha, Natysha, and Seth to bed. I backed our Jeep as close to the fire as I could, and got ready to turn the tape player on.

With everything ready, I played the tape for Deb.

When I listened to Tom and Alane's tapes, I liked what I heard about what they called a "wilderness experience." I even wanted to try it. However, I had about zero interest in going out to visit Tom and Alane. So when Dwight asked me, I told him "No" in a hurry.

"You can go," I said firmly, "but I'm not. Why would I want to go all the way to Montana to visit some people I don't even know?"

"Going out to see them is the last thing I want to do," I went on. "The tapes are always great, but when you see them in person, it's a big letdown."

But, as you probably know from reading this much of our book, Dwight can be rather convincing. So after awhile I started trying to think of the whole thing as our family's chance for a little longer vacation, since we hadn't had one in a long time. God even worked out the plane tickets, so we could fly our whole family to Montana and back for a very good price.

So off to Montana we went, and I have to admit I really did have a good time. Tom and Alane were very nice, and it encouraged me to see they were living practical and principled Christian lives. Their children were very nice, too, and I enjoyed watching how helpful they were in the kitchen as well as how cheerfully they helped with the chores.

I liked it out there in Montana. In fact, I thought Montana was the place God would have us to move to. So Tom and I rode around and looked at some property. I didn't say much to Deb about it, because her thoughts were not yet in that direction.

At that point, we didn't realize Tom and Alane were starting a ministry out of helping families like our own. People who were trying to slow down the pace of their lives, grow closer to God, or accomplish other worthy goals. We had just come to Montana to see how they lived. Toward the end of our visit when they asked us if we had any questions, we answered, "No."

"Did you find what you came here for?" they wondered. They wanted to know if our trip had a purpose besides being a vacation. When we told them we just wanted to observe them, they were truly surprised and not a little off-balance. They weren't used to being "observed," with few questions. But their example really encouraged us as we worked toward making additional changes in our own lives.

We hadn't been at Tom's for more than a few days when he asked me if we would enjoy visiting his friends Jim and Sally Hohnberger who lived "across the mountain." Jim and Sally were the reason the Water's family had moved to Montana. The tapes that Tom gave me—about wilderness living—were messages from both families. I remembered how Tom had said he would have to ask Alane, and I thought I would turn the tables on him a little.

So I told him I'd ask Deb about it, but my heart did not want to go at all. I felt safe, sure that Deb would say "no" and get me off the hook. So when I asked Deb about visiting the Hohnbergers, I was shocked when she said "Yes."

"But we don't even know them, Deb," I argued.

"Well, I came all the way out to Montana to see people I don't know," Deb replied. "Why wouldn't I go across a mountain to visit more people I don't know?" I couldn't argue with her reasoning, so we went. We didn't know it at the time, but we were in for a little adventure.

Tom explained to us that there were two ways to

get from his house to Jim's. We could drive three hours around a mountain, or thirty miles across a mountain pass on a very narrow road. We would have only one problem with the "pass option": we wouldn't be able to drive all the way across. So Tom would take us up as far as the snow would allow it on one side and we would walk across to meet Jim on the other.

We decided to take the shorter route, so Tom drove us up until his 4-wheel drive literally got stuck in the snow. Just as we finished digging Tom out, Jim appeared over the ridge of the mountain. So we loaded the children (ages 3, 4 and 9) and our luggage on the sleds, waved "Goodbye" to Tom, and waded across a mile of hip-deep snow with Jim.

Now, I didn't know it then, but Jim was really impressed that I didn't complain along the way. Here I was trudging through snow up to my hips and beyond, and he just thought I might have started complaining. But the snow-capped mountains overwhelmed me, and my eyes were busy drinking in the beauty of the woods, the wilderness, and the total seclusion.

"Deb certainly could be a mountain woman," Jim later whispered to Dwight.

In spite of our misgivings about visiting Jim and Sally, getting across the mountain was a very positive thing for us. For starters, we had a real miracle happen during the trip. When Jim drove up to get us, he stopped his Toyota Land Cruiser near the top of the pass. He had stopped at this point because his tires started to spin, even though he could have gone further with snow chains he felt impressed this was far enough. So he walked the remaining mile to meet us, and we walked back with him.

When we came around the bend and saw the Land Cruiser, we noticed there was a large fallen tree not more than six inches from Jim's bumper. But Deb and I assumed Jim had stopped there

145

because he didn't have a chain saw. But Jim knew differently.

"Wow, isn't that a miracle," he kept saying as we walked closer and closer to his truck. He then explained that the tree had fallen in the hour or so it took him to bring us back. Obviously, if Jim had driven six inches farther, that tree would have done serious damage to his truck. If he had driven 20 feet further, we would have been blocked in—20 miles from the nearest civilization with 3 children and nothing to do but walk down the mountain.

We believe God helped Jim to stop where he did so that tree would be in front of, not behind or on top of, his truck. It was just one more piece of evidence to us of God's watchful care and leading in our lives.

It had been a cloudy day, but as we rode down the mountain with Jim the clouds broke away. That's when we caught our first glimpse of the huge Rocky Mountains with their 10,000-foot peaks. And we were in awe; it was so beautiful. You couldn't see the Rockies from Tom's house, even though there were mountains. But this side of the mountain was truly incredible.

"Wow," I started to think. "I could live here!" And when I found out that the area we were in was 70 miles from town—40 of which were gravel road—I was even more excited.

"If we move out here, Dwight will have to slow down," I thought. "Just think—no power, no phones. Nothing but pine trees and mountains and us. Maybe these gravel roads will even make him drive slower!"

Dwight had the reputation of being a very fast driver. He simply had to pass everybody. And as I would later learn when we moved to Montana, it would take more than a gravel road to slow Dwight down. If a cloud of dust loomed ahead, he had to catch up with it just to pass it.

As God Leads the Way

It's hard to describe how Deb and I felt when the clouds broke away and we got our first glimpse of those mountains. It was so beautiful. The mountains on Tom's side were lovely—with trees going all the way to the top. But these were the 10,000-foot peaks, and they were truly awesome. I had been talking to Tom and Jim about what they called a "wilderness experience," like the one Moses had. And I wondered if God could work with me out here, helping me to take time to learn the principles that I really needed to learn. I knew it would be hard from the get-go, but I was a fighter. I had worked hard before, putting every ounce of effort I had into building our company. Now, with God's help, I wanted to put that same level of effort and even more into building a relationship with Him. To learn how to walk with Him, like I had never walked before. Here, in the midst of these gorgeous peaks with their snowy summits and tree-filled valleys, seemed like a truly magnificent place to learn more about and grow closer to my God.

Because I was getting serious about making a move, I asked Jim to show me some real estate. It made perfect sense to ask him, since he was a realtor like Tom.

"Well," Jim replied, "I want to be very careful." He wanted to help people learn the principles in those tapes, and worried that people would think his tapes were just a marketing tool to sell real estate. "I don't want to push real estate on anybody," Jim told me.

"Well, Jim," I replied, "you don't know me very well, but if I've decided I'm going to move out here and that's what God wants me to do, I will. So either you need to show me some real estate, or I need to find somebody else who will."

So Jim did show me some real estate, and by the time we left the Hohnbergers', Deb and I had made up our minds—we wanted to move to the wilderness of Montana. There would be a number of things to do before we could make the move, like selling our home and the business, and tying up other loose ends in Coldwater. But the more we prayed about it, the more we felt impressed to move out to the wilderness. As we traveled back to Michigan, we determined to pray and work in that direction.

Gems of Thought

When I thought about how God has so many people to watch after, and yet He concerned Himself with our wellbeing up there on that mountain pass, it really meant something to me. He cares about the sparrow that falls from the sky. He certainly cares about all the details in our life.

28

Called to the Wilderness

When Deb and I told our families about our wilderness plans, they were understandably less than enthusiastic. They loved us. They loved our children. They didn't want us to move away. It was hard for us, too, because we were very close to our families.

In spite of these misgivings, I knew I needed to make a move. When I read the Bible story of Moses, I realized that he needed a slower pace, change in surroundings, and time for communion with God. He needed time to learn to be reverent, humble and patient. As I studied his life and the experiences of other Bible characters that were called to a wilderness experience, I knew I needed that, too.

It's not that easy just to "pull up roots" and move into the wilderness. Selling our home was one of the biggest obstacles we faced. My mother did not think we would get our asking price for the house and land, and she did not think it was such a grand idea for us to move, anyway.

"Dwight," I remember her counseling, "I don't think you'll get what you want out of the property. But if God wants you to move, you will get your price—and not a penny less."

I got a lot of different responses when I told people we were moving so we could have a wilderness experience.

Some of our family and friends thought we were crazy. We

already lived in the country. We had a beautiful home in the middle of 160 acres, complete with a spring-fed pond and fish-filled channel. A large swamp sat on our property, with plenty of Canadian geese, muskrat, deer, and lots of birds.

But while our home was certainly in a secluded location, it wasn't a wilderness experience for me.

"Dwight," our pastor advised, "your problem is that you need to give more Bible studies."

"How can I give more Bible studies," I quipped. "I don't even have time for the ones I'm giving now."

"You need to be more involved in the church," said others. "You are not busy enough for the Lord."

But I was already so very busy in the church. And I wanted to know, "What more can I do?"

I needed more time with my family. Until this time, my family was always left out. I was never home. My kids hardly knew me.

I remember seeing a TV news clip where a lady said the average father spends only 43 seconds per day with his children. I thought in my mind, Come on! That's ridiculous. I thought the woman to be biased—she had something against fathers. But I want to tell you something, certainly not to my credit, but only to my embarrassment. I checked it out, and the lady was right.

When I got home from work everyday, my three children would run up to hug and kiss me.

"Daddy, Daddy, I'm so glad to see you," they would ramble. Then they wanted to play.

"Not right now, not right now." I would refuse. "I've got to eat."

As soon as we got done eating they would say, "We want to play." I would say, "Let's have a little worship." Then after worship, on went the TV to the news or something and I would say, "Not right now, don't bother me."

Before I knew it they would be in bed. In my heart, I knew I didn't even spend 20 seconds with my children each day.

And I wanted to change all that. To put my life into slow

motion for awhile, spend a lot of time with my wife and children, and really get to know my God.

When life becomes very complex, it's not easy to make it "uncomplicated." We know, because it took us nine months to "tie up" the loose ends and get ready to move to the wilderness. But in the end and with God's help, we did accomplish it. And at last, with the last garage sale behind us, we loaded what remained of our belongings into a Ryder truck I had bought and headed west—west toward the wilderness of Montana.

Gems of Thought
When life becomes very complex, it's not easy to make it "uncomplicated." But, I wanted to slow down so that I could hear that still small voice. I wanted to get away from the pace and distractions of everyday life, and really get to know my family and my God.

29

Smoothing Rough Edges

Before we moved into the wilderness, I made a list of my "besetting sins." These were weaknesses I had struggled with for many years without gaining the victory. Then I confessed those sins to God.

"Lord," I prayed, "I need to slow down. I'm too busy. I never spend enough time with my children and my wife, especially any quality time."

I also confessed that while I spent a lot of time in Bible study, I didn't really know how to commune with God, and I wanted to do that.

Financially, our marriage had been somewhat of a roller coaster experience. We didn't have much when we first got married. Unfortunately, we were also inclined to spend what we made rather freely. So for a while, we never really got ahead. Only when we were in Tulsa did we make a new start financially. Along with our recommitment to Christ, we also made a commitment to pay a faithful tithe. In addition, we began to set aside a faithful 10% for ourselves.

In the early days of our marriage, Deb would "nickel and dime" our budget while I would go out and spend hundreds of dollars at a time. By the time we decided to make a major change, we were in debt big-time. Our credit cards were filled up, and we could hardly make it from week to week. During this time, there were moments that even if we needed a pair of socks, we wouldn't buy them because the money just wasn't there.

Our financial situation began to improve when we made a pact between ourselves: we would not go out and buy anything unless we told each other about it, and waited one week. While this policy was difficult at times, it worked. We firmly believe in debt-free living, and have taught our children that if they don't have the money to buy something, it's better to wait until they do.

I also could not control my temper or my passions. I loved my wife—until the moment she crossed my will. Then I let her have it. I told her exactly where she stood. And I knew I needed to change all of this.

I also needed to simplify. My life was much too busy. I needed to sort the details of my life, and bring it into order.

Then I had a problem with "evil surmising." Also, my faith was weak—so weak that it was actually an idol to me. So many times I would make excuses for myself, saying, "Well, I'm not perfect, I have to have some weaknesses."

When we moved to Montana, I knew that overcoming these temptations would be hard, but I also knew God promised to be with me. I knew I was going into the wilderness to do training—just like basic training for the Airborne Rangers.

Thankfully, the wilderness we moved to was not a hot and barren desert. In fact, we could see the Rocky Mountains right out the window, not to mention moose and bear and many other types of wildlife. But while the scenery was incredibly eye-catching, I didn't move out to Montana for the sheer splendor of it. I went to spend time with God. To learn of Him, and have Him show His will to me.

I wish I could say that I changed overnight when I moved to Montana, but that's hardly the case. I brought all my besetting sins with me right to Montana, and so did my wife and children.

Through this experience, I learned that change does take time. It took me 34 years to become the way I was. I had worked hard everyday to become that person, and I didn't unlearn my bad habits overnight.

As I studied the Bible in a new way, I realized that Moses spent 40 years in the wilderness, John the Baptist spent nearly 30, and that David herded sheep for a number of years while preparing to be king. Even Paul, as much as he knew when he was converted, spent three years in the Arabian desert (Galatians 1:17, 18). So I didn't expect the wilderness to work some kind of magic.

I would truly make the choice to allow God to change me. I knew He had the power, but because of His great love, He never forces the will. It is up to us to make the choice and keep making the choice. It is called surrender, something I only knew in theory, but not in actual experimentation. Oh God, I kept saying. Help me to be willing. I know it's the little things that have tripped me up.

As I drove the truck with my family and all our earthly goods toward Montana, I didn't know what all those "little things" would be. But by God's grace I did determine that now, with His help, things would be different.

Gems of Thought

I am not advocating that we should go around telling people that we're perfect. But we should be, as the Bible says, striving to "enter in at the strait gate" (Luke 13:24). And when we make excuses for our weaknesses, what we are really saying is that God doesn't have the power to help us be overcomers. Therefore, Satan has more power than God does.

I used to wear a T-shirt when I was a kid that said, "The Devil Made Me Do It." When I figured out what it was really saying, I threw it away. I realize now that the devil cannot make me do anything. He can tempt me, but I have a choice.

As I've traveled from place to place speaking, I have realized that many other people shared in the weaknesses I had. In fact, quite a few have come up to me after I shared my story and said, "Dwight, you and I have a lot in common." That's because I'm a fairly common person.

30

Taming the TV

Back in Coldwater, the television had been a major problem in our home. Although I never cared to watch TV myself, Dwight was really into it, especially the TV program "M*A*S*H. You couldn't talk to him at all when he was watching TV; he was that engrossed. When things got really exciting you could even see Dwight's heart pumping, right through his shirt!

Before we moved to Montana, we decided that the TV must go. We didn't want our children to watch that stuff, and we just needed to get away from the set entirely.

Now that I have given my life to Jesus, it seems to me that TV and many of the programs on it exist to take your mind away from spiritual things. And television is so much worse today than when I was young. For example, I remember when the married stars of "I Love Lucy" slept in separate beds. Today, even G-rated and Walt Disney movies have couples in bed. More than that, many things they show don't leave much more for the mind to imagine.

Many educators feel they have to tell the students about "safe sex." But they shouldn't have to do that, and they wouldn't, if there weren't so many vulgar movies and TV programs and video games affecting our children today. What many of us don't understand is that Satan always mixes good with bad. He is a master at confusing us.

I have found out through my experiences that Satan does this in two ways that most of us all fall into.

One, he excites our passions and appetites. If we are honest with ourselves, many of us know we don't eat like we should. Once the devil clouds the mind so we don't hear that still small voice he has gained a big victory. Here is a scenario that many people are caught up in. They don't eat well all day because of time and then when they get home they fix their big meal, sit down and watch the TV. This is certainly not God's plan.

The other is time. He has us so busy that we don't have time to make good decisions. Most of us just go with the flow.

Because there are some good programs on TV, some people feel we shouldn't have gotten rid of it. But is that a good reason to watch television? There may be something good in arsenic, but I don't take it. There will always be good mixed with the bad.

For myself, I decided that I had to get rid of the TV, to flee from temptation. Even if I spend two hours watching a program that is "really not that bad" and even has some sort of spiritual application, my time would be better spent with the Bible or other more rewarding activities such as visiting someone or spending time with my family rather than being entertained.

We wanted our entertainment "taste buds" to change. So we got rid of it before we even moved.

While we realize that not everyone may be able to move to the country, we did find the country life very helpful to us spiritually. And we do believe that country life is something everyone should strive for, before every other enjoyment.

"And why is country living so important?" you may ask. Because of the simple Biblical principle: "by beholding we become changed" (paraphrase of 2 Corinthians 3:18). When we lived in Tulsa, there were spotlights out at night, together with helicopters and other police vehicles looking for thieves and murderers. Then there were all the billboards with scantily clad women, or cigarettes, or alcohol. It all has an effect on us sooner or later. As the old saying goes, "Garbage in, garbage out."

If you work in a construction environment where everybody cusses and swears all day, pretty soon, if you aren't careful you may be swearing, too. In your efforts to lead a pure and holy life, it is important to keep yourself and your children as far away from that type of environment as you can. By living close to nature, we were able to escape the bombardment of billboards, sirens, music, and other junk.

It's one thing when you have to go into that kind of environment to do your shopping, banking, or whatever. But if you can make a move or change your circumstances to avoid harmful environments, by all means do it. We need to stop making excuses, and realize that we are tying God's hands when we don't do the good things we need to do.

When we got rid of the TV, we pretty much did it cold turkey. But when we took the TV away from our children, we replaced it with other things. We did a lot more together as a family, like cutting wood for our heat, special projects, etc. Then when we did get a TV again, we kept it in the closet. You had to physically take it out if you wanted to watch anything. We only used it on rare occasions when we would get a nature video. This was a special treat. As our children have gotten older, we have noticed that it is a shock to them when they are exposed to some of the things on TV, and this is good. We did not want them to become used to those things.

Music was another big temptation to me. I was really into rock and roll, but when I gave my heart fully to Christ I knew from experience that I could not be close to Christ if I listened to that music. So I gladly gave it up.

Today, I believe that music is one of the biggest problems facing our young people. Music is a language, and a powerful one at that. If it weren't, they would not play such scary music in so many movie scenes. Take away the music and the movie isn't nearly as gripping. Yet with the music you know there is danger right away, even without the words.

Some people say, "Well, I know this music is bad, but I like it." But that argument is about as good as saying "I know this food is bad for me, but it tastes good so I'm going to eat it anyway." We need to make the decision not to eat or listen or watch those things that are bad for us. We can make these changes. We start by deciding to make a change. Then we take it one day at a time. That's what I did with my drinking habit. These decisions are made out of principle, not because something feels good. Satan is a master at working on our senses—at making things look, feel and sound good. In contrast, when we have the mind of Christ, we make decisions out of principle. This is not to say we don't have emotions; in fact, Christ had emotions. But when Paul said, "Let this mind be in you, which was also in Christ Jesus", he was telling us to work out of principle (Philippians 2:5).

Each day we can say "By God's grace I make the decision today." We are not to worry about tomorrow. When I quit drinking, "forever" seemed like such a long time. So I took one day at a time. And I didn't keep alcohol around the house to tempt me, either. That would have only been an open invitation to failure. God will give us the power to win the victory if we do our part, which is to make a decision and then act upon it.

Every morning when we choose to get up, we are making this kind of a choice. We could set our alarm and pray, "Lord, please help me to get up in the morning." But unless we make a conscious decision to get up when the alarm rings, chances are good that we won't. Breaking habits takes more than desire; it takes a decision. We are told that many will be lost while hoping and desiring to be Christians (Matthew 7:21). So we have a choice to make.

"How long halt ye between two opinions?" Elijah questioned the Israelites when they gathered on Mt. Carmel (1Kings 18:21). As Christians, we are challenged to "choose you this day whom ye will serve" (Joshua 24:15). For us, "taming the TV" was an important part of that process. "For where your treasure is, there will your heart be also" (Matthew 6:21).

Gems of Thought

Some people might hear our story and think they need to have a wilderness experience before they can take care of these things. But not everyone can move off to Montana, Timbuktu, or wherever. So we need to start having a wilderness experience, and take care of these things as we are convicted about them, right now. We must quit making excuses, acting in faith as God shows us what to do. As the famous text says, "Now is accepted time, now is the day of salvation" (paraphrase of 2 Corinthians 6:2).

Let's say you were to do a triathlon (an athletic event) in which participants compete without stopping in three successive events, usually long distance running, long distance swimming, and long distance bicycling. If you have ever done this, or watched the event, you know it is not easy. The participants train a long time before they actually compete. During training, they watch very carefully what they eat. They make sure they get enough rest. In other words, while in training they take every advantage they can. They have one chance to win.

As Christians, we are in training. It is called character development. We have only one lifetime to get ready, and who knows how long that life will last? In my quest to walk with God, I have found that every advantage we take is to our benefit. Believe me. It makes all the difference in the world. We think that is the best way for dealing with most any temptation to sin, when we are convicted that something we do is wrong, is to stop it right away. Smokers who try to quit gradually usually fail. While gradual changes may be in order for some areas like diet, Jesus didn't tell the harlot to "cut down" on her activities. He told her to "go and sin no more."

31

Getting "Down to Speed"

Life in Montana was certainly different from the "rat race" experience I had lived prior to the move. It was life in the slow lane—packed with plenty of lessons for my family and myself. In the wilderness, I found time to do things that I had never been able to do before. Like finding four leaf clovers.

As a child, I searched the fields in vain for a four-leaf clover. It's hard to believe now, but it took me 35 years to find my first four-leaf clover. And I found it in Montana, with my children. They were so excited, and so was I. Now we have a whole display of four-leaf clovers in our home. And we also have five-leaf, six-leaf, and even a seven-leaf clover!

Oh, it took time to find those clovers. But I took time with my family in Montana. And I started to realize that the very first work that we have is with our families. In fact, nothing should take precedence over this.

In Mark 8:36 we read "what doth it profit a man if he gain the whole world, and lose his own soul?" In the wilderness, I had to be honest with myself. I had been gaining things of the world, but losing my own soul. I had called myself a Christian—talked the talk, so to speak, but I hadn't walked the walk. Unknown to me I was doing the same thing I had condemned others for doing.

For example, I used to tell my family that I loved them, and I did. I even showed them by buying things for them. As I started to make changes, I came to the stark realization that they wanted me, not the things I could buy. It took me 35 years to find my first four-leaf clover, but praise God I did it. It's never too late to redeem the time.

Mail delivery was another highlight of life in the country. In the wilderness of Montana, mail came only twice a week. On Tuesdays and Fridays, to be exact. Now back in Michigan, when I did not have time for anything, I could not have cared less about the mail. Things were different in Montana, however. When the mail came it was a main event. We went and picked it up as a family, not opening anything until we were all in the house. As we opened each letter, we read it as a family, and it was a real low if we didn't get anything.

When we lived in Michigan, I was always gone. But when we moved to Montana, I was always home.

Before we moved, Deb used to say to me, "Dwight, I can't wait until we can spend a lot more time together out in the wilderness. We'll never be separated!" But it was not too long after we moved to Montana when she started saying, "Wow! We're always together! This is really different."

One of my weaknesses that "moved" with me to Montana was the bad habit of always being in a rush, and arriving at every destination in just the nick of time.

In Montana, 40 or 50 miles of gravel road separated us from the nearest town. After driving the way I did for so many years, I wasn't about to let that gravel road slow me down. No. Not me. If there was a straightaway and I could go 75 miles per hour, I did. In fact, it turned into kind of a race. I would get into town and exclaim, "Wow, Deb, I made it in 63 minutes this time. I wonder what I can do on the way home."

As I hurtled along, I often saw my wife trying to slam on the brake from the passenger side. Of course, there was no brake! So then she would resort to squeezing my leg, but it only seemed to make me go faster. It all seems kind of humorous to me now, but looking back on the way I really was, it was bad, very bad.

Like he said, Dwight didn't slow down overnight. Although he finally did slow down, it took awhile. Believe it or not, before we left Montana he drove so slow the kids were saying, "Oh, we're never going to get to town" and "He's going so slow!"

Dwight also took a lot more time with the children in Montana. He spent time with them on their personal problems, instead of just letting me handle it all. Of course, this was made easier by the fact that there was no peer pressure out in the wilderness. We didn't have to keep up with the Jones' kids, because we were by ourselves. Our kids did not even know what name brand clothing was. As a result, we saved thousands of dollars by buying nice clothes that fit—without having to keep up with Johnny or Susie.

This does not mean that we became hermits. We had friends out in Montana, and we often got together for church or other special occasions. But it was that competitive, time-oriented, city-like pace of life we so much enjoyed getting rid of.

It got easier to be relaxed about things and not nearly so competitive out in the country. I remember when Alysha was born, we were so anxious for her to do well. We wanted her to walk among her little "peers," be the first to say her ABCs, etc. In fact, we taught Alysha her ABCs when she was only two! And we really enjoyed it when people commented, "Isn't she a smart little girl?" or "Isn't she sharp!"

But as we started to think about these things, we realized that we did not want our family to grow up so fast. We began to see that our children would grow up before we hardly knew what had happened, and that we should slow down and "smell the roses" along with them. We wanted to enjoy this job of bringing our children up, and do it ourselves, rather than having them raised by a school or a daycare center.

Getting Down to Speed

During this time, our family came to enjoy meals in a way we never had before. We actually sat down as a family and ate together, and we all looked forward to it. In addition, because we didn't have a TV to entertain them, the children learned to be quite creative in the things they did.

While we were in Montana we started celebrating "just because" days, which were days we did something special "just because" we loved each other. Sometimes we would "honor" one of the children on a "just because" day. For example, if it were Natysha's special day she would get to pick what we had for dinner. She wouldn't have to help fix or clean up after the meal, either. Then after the meal, we would all sit down and tell Natysha why we cared about her. Just because, you know. Because we loved her.

Personally, I much prefer a "Just Because" day to Valentine's Day, Sweetest Day, or all those other commercially-oriented days when you are supposed to do something special for someone you love. I do not like being told when to get a card, flowers, or treat for my wife. This doesn't mean I don't like to do anything for them, it just means that I like to do a special surprise because I wanted to, not because somebody set up a day. This practice also helps us to think for ourselves to do things not because society has programmed us to do it, but because we took the time to think.

Our kids really enjoyed the surprises we did for them, and because they liked the "just because" idea, they really got into doing special things for us, too. They especially liked to fix meals, and so many times they set up the card table with candles and flowers and served us something special. They actually enjoyed serving their parents, and coming up with "surprises" that most kids wouldn't be interested in today.

Sometimes they put on little plays for us, and once for our anniversary they had me put on my wedding dress. They had Dwight dress in white pants and a shirt, and made little yellow bow ties for him and Seth. Dwight had to stand at the bottom of the stairs and wait for me. Then Alysha, 12 years old at the time, played the wedding song while I came down, all dressed in my wedding gown.

They got out all the wedding things we had—candles, glasses and the whole works, and gave us a surprise "reception." They prepared an entire meal, complete with three or four courses. Then Alysha played some other wedding songs on the piano for us. We were amazed at how creative and fun the children could be, and it was all very special.

I think children really like to do things for their parents; in fact, they long to. But so often they get shoved out of the way because the parents are just too busy. So the kids get wrapped up in other kids, and it is usually not a good influence. The children then bond with other children instead of their parents, and that is how they get into trouble. Our children had bonded with Deb through the years, but not so much with me. In Montana, much more of this bonding took place. I found it really neat to take time with the kids, and frankly, I felt very honored to have them love me the way they did.

Time really seemed to slow down for us in Montana. When you live a fast-paced life, it seems like things happen so quickly. But our children were "kids" for a long time, and they didn't seem to grow up too quickly. I think it was because of the slower pace of life. As parents it's easy to think our kids will always be with us. Yet in many cases, we only have them for 16 or 18 years. Then they are off to college, or simply busy forging a new life of their own. It is so important for us to take time with them when they are young, because we will not have such an opportunity later.

Getting Down to Speed

Of course, everything wasn't perfect in Montana. When we made the move, I packed my terrible temper up, took it right along with me, and had a desperate struggle with it. One case in point: when we were building our home.

We bought a Ryder truck for the move, because I intended to turn it into a flatbed and work with it when we were done. One day I needed some steel and insulation for the house. Because we lived so far away, going into town was a big family outing. So Deb and the children rode with me to pick up the needed supplies. We did not get all our shopping done that day, so we decided to stay overnight in a motel and finish up the next day.

I went to lock the door of the Ryder truck, only to find that the padlock was missing. Dusk faded into moonlight, and I didn't have a flashlight, so I tried to look for the padlock by whatever glimmer I could get.

When the lock did not turn up quickly, I started to get frustrated. To make matters worse, I ripped my good ski jacket on a metal piece of the truck. Down feathers flew everywhere and I went flying, too—into a rage, that is. I started slamming things around and throwing insulation all over the place.

During this entire episode, my wife and children just stood there looking at me as if I were some sort of a crazy person. And then, right then, is when the still small voice started speaking to me again.

"Dwight, this is what you are here for," it said. "You'll never make it into the kingdom of heaven acting like this. There's only one thing, Dwight that you can take into the kingdom of heaven, and that's your character. You know. Your thoughts and your feelings."

"You can't take your house, your car, your money, or even the body you've got right now. So where is your treasure, Dwight? You need to learn of me, and that's why you're here in the wilderness. Because I can't trust you the way you are right now."

Right at that moment, I paid little attention to the still small voice. I just kept throwing things.

165

"Don't you think you ought to calm down, Dwight?" my wife finally asked.

I told her to be quiet, but boy was I rebuked in my heart. Later I apologized. It became clear to me then, clearer than ever, how much I needed to change.

I'll never forget that incident with the Ryder truck. Dwight was in the bed of the truck, just acting like an animal.

"Now, children," I would explain to the kids whenever Dwight flew off the handle like that. "Daddy really doesn't want to act this way, but he doesn't know what he's doing right now. But you don't ever want to act this way, because it's wrong."

Dwight had no control of anything back then, but I guess it really hit him when he saw us watching him like that. He said later that when he saw us all watching him so calmly from outside the truck, he felt like an animal in a cage. Something happened in his mind that night. He knew he needed to change.

Gems of Thought

I did need to change, and God showed that to me clearly, which leads me to a question: how do you (as a reader) relate to all of this? How do you treat your children? Are you fair with your employer? Or do you put down that you left work at such and such a time, and then leave five minutes early? Do you feel like you are doing everything God has asked you to do? Or do you need a personal wilderness experience?

I didn't write this book just to have nice stories for people to read. Oh no. I wrote it because of a burden on my heart to help others to get their hearts right, and by faith be in the kingdom. Part of getting there is to understand our true spiritual condition. We are not to make excuses for our weaknesses, for Jesus says our very weaknesses can become strengths if we will only give them to Him.

If a movie camera lay hidden in a corner of your house, taping you all week long, what kind of scenes would it take? If the pastor of your church were to ask you to play those movies for church next weekend for an example of what a Christian wife or husband or family would be, what would you say? Would you be happy to have him play that movie, or would you be offering rather large sums of money—whatever it took—to keep those "highlights" off the screen?

Pure and transparent characters—that's what Jesus wants us to be. The more transparent we become, the more of Jesus people will see each day as they look at us. Then we wouldn't mind it if the pastor did want to show a movie of what we did or ate or said in a day, because people would only see Jesus in every aspect of our lives. I learned these lessons, one by one, through my own experience. God showed me that it is possible to be a church elder, even a pastor, head elder, Sabbath (or Sunday) school teacher, deacon or deaconess, and not even be close to the heavenly kingdom because you have not surrendered your soul to Christ. That it is possible to do a great work, and yet have a heart that is miserable and poor and wretched. And I didn't want to be that way any more.

32

From the Inside Out

Before my "wilderness experience," I always thought my weaknesses would someday just "go away." But unfortunately, they seemed to just get worse instead.

It was like that in my marriage, too. On the outside Deb and I could put on "smiley" faces and it even looked like we got along. But in our hearts, it was quite a different story.

·I always said I loved my wife, and I did very much. I always said I would do anything for her. When I said that, to me it meant climbing the tallest mountain or swimming the biggest ocean. You know; something big. When we moved to Montana and my wife asked me if I could help do the dishes or help can fruit, love took on a new meaning.

Before we went to Montana we were a typical family. We looked good on the outside, like we were really getting along. But when we got home from the party or church outing, it was nothing to get into an argument about something stupid.

When you are dating, it seems like you think about all the "big" things. But after you get married, it's the little things that mess you up. Like putting the top on the toothpaste after you use it.

When we first got married, Dwight would get so

irritated because I did not put a lid on the toothpaste. I couldn't see why it was any big deal, since I planned to use the toothpaste again anyway. But it was a big deal to Dwight. I wish I could say I started putting the lid on right away to please Dwight, but that's not the way it was. But I did get around to changing my habit, after awhile.

Another thing that really bothered Dwight was the fact that he always wiped the sink out after he brushed his teeth, and I didn't. These things seem kind of dumb now, but they can really grind on you, and we used to argue about them, too. But in Montana, we took time to deal with all these "little" issues. We confronted them, and then chose to change them, accept them, or at the very least understand why each of us did what we did.

When I was younger, I hated doing the dishes with a passion. So much so, in fact, that I would pay my brothers a dollar just to take my turn. And when I got married, I figured that washing dishes was my wife's job. I simply wasn't doing any of that "stuff."

But when we moved to Montana, I decided to start helping with the dishes. The first time I picked up a dishrag, my children were so surprised it actually embarrassed me. Deb rubbed her eyes a couple of times, making sure it was Dwight Hall. In fact, she thought it such a momentous occasion that she got out the video camera and took a picture just to make sure that yes, this really was happening. Even though I still do not do them very often, the willingness principle is what prevails. It is the surrendering of self that made this possible.

We were all shocked when Dwight picked up a dishrag. I mean, he is not the kind of guy who even knows where the silverware drawer is, and I didn't expect him to. Dwight always says that if necessary, he can get his own granola and apple juice. But I'm not even sure about that.

If I was really on a time limit and needed some help, he would have helped. But I always figured taking care of the kitchen was my role, so I didn't expect anything from him there, although it was really nice when he started to help.

I helped can fruit, too, and for the first time in my married life, I actually made family time a real priority—although it did not come easily or naturally for me.

Some days keeping my priorities straight was a real struggle. On one particular day I had my agenda completely planned. I was in a hurry to have family worship, eat, and start working outside. But my children had their own plans for my morning.

"Mom, Dad, would you please go back upstairs and get in bed?" they asked. "We've got something special planned for you this morning."

"Well, I've already got my work clothes on," I started in. I had already been up since 5:00 a.m. With both personal and family devotions cared for, I just wanted to get a bowl of cereal and start cutting wood.

"Oh, please Daddy," they begged. And that still small voice was whispering in my ear again.

"Dwight—what are you here for?"

So I listened to the still small voice, went upstairs and climbed into bed. Then the children came in with a pen and paper.

"Welcome to our restaurant!" they said cheerily. "And what can we get you for breakfast this morning?"

I did not try to hide that I was in a hurry, and my order reflected it.

"I'll just have some cereal," I told the children, "and if you can do it quite quickly, you can add some toast." What I really wanted was just to get this over with so I could get on with my day.

But my wife, she was a different story. She didn't have a

whole lot to do that day compared to me, or so I thought. She quite enjoyed the thought of having breakfast in bed. In fact, she loved it.

"Well now, what do you have on your menu?" Deb asked the kids.

"Come on, Deb," I was thinking. "Just hurry up!" But Deb didn't listen to my thoughts, of course. She was too busy pondering the rather detailed and lengthy list of menu options. In fact, she was having a hard time deciding between them.

"Well, I'm not sure," she said several times. "Maybe I'll have pancakes, or no, maybe I'll have some muffins instead."

Now as you can imagine, my Type A personality wasn't ready for this type of delay at all. But the entire time that still small voice kept whispering in my ear. "Dwight—what are you here for?" So I listened as Deb ordered a combination of tasty menu items that would undoubtedly take much longer to fix than my simple cereal and toast.

When the orders were made and the "cooks" went down to the kitchen I turned to Deb, making no effort to hide my irritation. "Deb, you know I need to get outside and cut that wood. I don't have too much time left. You could have helped me out. We could have done this 'just because' at a more convenient date."

"I hope they hurry up and get this done."

"Dwight, they very seldom do this," she replied. Then the clincher—"What are we here for, anyway?"

"Yeah, you're right," I replied.

Dwight was really in a big hurry that day. He wanted to get outside to cut wood or something. But the kids had other plans, of course.

When I place an order at a restaurant, I want to know what my choices are. I mean, they may have made muffins or something and if that's available, I want to try it. But Dwight was kind of hitting my leg, saying "Hurry up, I don't have time for this." And I told him to take it easy, the woods would still be there waiting for him when he was done. But he was getting a little excited about it all.

It was a tremendous breakfast the children fixed, and I truly did enjoy it. But as we neared the end of the meal, I started thinking again of my well-laid plans for the day. And I was anxious to get things started.

Little did I realize that God had another lesson to teach me that morning before I would get to do what I thought I needed to do. I was slowly learning to listen, but my attitude was still a long way off. It was a lesson in parenting, and patience.

Gems of Thought

We needed to find the principle through the Bible to have the right foundation, not that we had to be right, but that we would choose to do right according to Biblical principle. We soon learned that kneeling together in prayer was the best way to resolve both our big and little differences. Together we asked God for strength and courage to do what was right. I read in *Patriarchs and Prophets* (part of *The Bible Study Companion Set*) that Eve was so close to Adam that she was his "second self." The biggest battle we ever have to fight is with our own self, but what is the second biggest battle? It is with my spouse—my second self—because she reveals so many things to me that I know I need to change. When I stopped trying to protect myself, and realized that my spouse was the best teacher I had, Deb and I found that we were not enemies! Indeed, we loved and still do love each other very much. Now we can work for each other's salvation, because we see each other in a positive rather than in a negative way.

33

What Are You Here For?

Just as Deb and I were finishing the delicious breakfast the children had prepared, Alysha (our oldest child), brought me a letter.

"What do you think of this, Dad?" she asked, her eyes big with anticipation, waiting for my response. After all, this was the first letter she had typed on her new "Star Writer." It was also a thank you note to her Uncle Wayne, who had bought the Star Writer for her in the first place.

"It took me all day yesterday to type this letter, Dad," Alysha said. "What do you think?"

As I read the letter, it didn't take me long to realize that, in spite of her efforts, Alysha had made a number of mistakes, and they were mistakes that she should have known about or could have corrected. In other words, it was less than her best.

She had misspelled some words that I knew she could spell, some of the sentences didn't start with a capital letter, and one even ran right off the edge of the page. This really bothered me, because in our homeschooling we had been studying how to do things "promptly, thoroughly and well." We all agreed that those were the principles we should follow. We had also talked about the neatness of Jesus, and how He had even folded his grave clothes when He arose from the dead (John 20:7). I had also told my family that God cares about the little things, and repeated to them the admonition of my grandmother, "If you learn to save the pennies, the dollars will take care of themselves." So I didn't feel like I should let this pass entirely. Yet I did not want to hurt Alysha, so I had no idea of what to say.

I could think of four or five excuses why I should not say a thing. After all, this was a new typewriter. Alysha had spent a whole day on the letter. I was in a hurry, and didn't have time to deal with it. In addition, I had just finished eating the delightful breakfast that Alysha helped to fix.

"What do you think, Dad?" Alysha persisted, and I felt so torn. I did not want to say anything, yet I felt that if I didn't, I would be undoing some of the lessons we had just learned. On top of that, I heard the still small voice saying, "Dwight, she's asked for your opinion. Are you going to tell the truth? And if you do, are you going to have the spirit of my son Jesus?" Then I knew what I needed to do.

"Alysha, there are some mistakes here," I said. I could feel Alysha's countance fall as she put her head down. In the meantime, my wife softly nudged my side. You know, one of those nudges that asks a husband, "How could you do something like this?"

By this time, Alysha had tears streaming down her face. "But Dad, I spent all day."

"Alysha, I know there are some mistakes in here that you didn't even know about," I told her, "and I would be glad to let those go, but there are some simple words here that I know you know how to spell." "And there are other mistakes I think you could have fixed."

"But I didn't know how to erase my mistakes," Alysha responded. "And I did spend all day on this letter. Besides, I didn't know how to save it and it will take me another day to redo it. I thought you would have said it was a good job."

My heart ached. I did want to say it was a good job. More than anything else, I wanted to make Alysha happy, be done with this conversation, and get started on the work I had planned for the day. Yet I knew that would not be right.

What Are You Here For

"You need to be honest, Dwight," I heard the still small voice whispering in my ear. "But you also need to be kind, and handle this in the spirit of Jesus." A struggle was going on in that room right then and there—the same struggle that goes on in our homes and churches so much of the time. For it is easier to talk behind a person's back than to deal with the issues. Satan constantly tries to get in the way to keep us from doing our best. "Jesus wants your best," I had taught my family. "He doesn't settle for mediocrity, and the enemy of best is good." I knew that, as gently but firmly as I could, I needed to address this issue.

"Well, you did ask me what I thought," I replied. "Did you want your father to tell the truth?"

"Yes," said Alysha, while Deb cast another meaningful glance in my direction that told me exactly where she stood. But while I couldn't lie, once again I heard that still small voice speaking to my heart: "Dwight, this is your wilderness experience for today."

"I'll tell you what, Alysha," I said. "I want you to go to your room and pray to God. Ask Him what you should do." I knew if I told her to type the letter again she would, for Alysha had always been obedient. But I didn't want her to do it because I told her to—I wanted her to do it because she realized it was right and chose to do it.

"Well," Alysha replied, "if I go to my room, I know what you want me to do. So if I say I don't want to redo it, then you're going to want me to do it over again regardless."

"No," I replied. "You go to your room and ask Jesus what He would want you to do under the circumstances. And if you decide not to change the letter, I promise not to say a thing."

So Alysha went, and a few minutes later she was back again.

"I did pray, and I've been thinking about how we've been learning to do things promptly, thoroughly and well," she said. "And as I prayed, God impressed me that I should do this letter over again."

"And you didn't make this decision because of me?" I asked.

"No," Alysha replied. "I decided myself." I could see the

175

peace in Alysha's face—that she was no longer irritated or fighting the idea. Instead, she was happy because she made the right decision. Of course, Deb and I were happy too. So I gave Alysha a hug, and told her I was happy about her decision.

"Dad, I don't know how to run that Star Writer very well," Alysha told me. "I didn't even save my letter in the memory, so now I have to start all over again."

"Well, when you have it out and ready, I will help you," I replied. Little did I know that she would get it around so quickly!

Then Seth and Natysha took our trays, and we said, "Thank you very much", and in my heart I said, "Now, I am going to go outside and work."

"Dwight, I was sure upset when you pointed out those mistakes to Alysha," Deb said as I headed out the bedroom door. "But now I'm so thankful you did."

Of course, those comments made me happy too. I appreciated how Deb stood behind me even when she wasn't sure about what I was doing. I also realized how bad it would have been if I had let things go just because I didn't want to hurt Alysha's feelings. That's what a lot of families do today, and their children get away with terrible things because we don't want to say anything to them. But I wanted to live by principles, to do what was best even if it did make for difficult conversation at times.

I didn't know it at the moment, but there was one more surprise in store for me that morning. Just as I was thanking God for helping me handle the Star Writer situation and heading toward the door to begin my work, I "ran into" Alysha in the dining room. Being the capable and efficient girl that she is, there she was—with the Star Writer all set up and ready to go.

"Dad, I've got it ready now," she was saying. "Can you help me?"

Can you imagine that? I just spent an extra hour and a half upstairs when I wanted to be outside, my day was literally ticking away, and now I have to spend more time on this Star Writer!

"I'm never going to get any work done today," I said to myself.

But once again that still small voice was whispering in my ear: "Dwight, what are you here for? Isn't your family the whole reason you are out here" and, "What is your most important work today, Dwight?"

And so I spent another two hours figuring out how to use the Star Writer, and Alysha spent all of her free time that day redoing that letter.

When she was done, she told her Uncle Wayne about redoing the letter. She said at first she thought her dad had been too hard on her, but then she had prayed and God impressed her to do it over. And Uncle Wayne told me later that Alysha's story about redoing the letter had really touched his heart.

When I finally did make it out to the woodpile, God really blessed. I believe He helped me get more wood cut that day than I thought I could, because I spent the time I needed to with Alysha.

Looking back on it now, I'm so thankful that I did not get upset or angry during that situation; that I was learning to listen to that still small voice and learning to walk with God. This whole story reminds me of a quote I have read many times, which means a lot to me:

"Every act of life, however small, has its bearing for good or for evil. Faithfulness or neglect in what are apparently the smallest duties may open the door for life's richest blessing or its greatest calamities. It is the little things that test the character. It is the unpretending acts of daily self-denial, performed with a cheerful willing heart, that God smiles upon." *Patriarchs and Prophets* (*Bible Study Companion Set*) 158

Gems of Thought

I began to realize that walking with God is not some magical something that we cannot get our hands around. Walking with God is a moment-by-moment surrender doing the things that lie nearest. Theological correctness is not the only thing that matters. We have to hold the truth in righteousness. Romans 1:18 says "For the wrath of God is revealed from heaven against all ungodliness and unrighteousness of men, who hold the truth in unrighteousness." In other words if we only know by theory and not by experience we are what I call lukewarm Christians and Revelation chapter 2 verse 16 gives us a view of what will happen to a lukewarm individual. Even as non-Christians we have a theory or head knowledge, what we should or should not do. But to put these principles in action, that is another story. We have got to get past theoretical knowledge.

34

The Power of a Simple Prayer

One lesson Dwight and I learned was the value of praying together. We learned that, as a Christian couple, we could not afford not to pray. We also learned that praying together and for each other was and still is the very best way to settle our disagreements. How well I remember the first time Dwight said, "Let's pray" right in the middle of a major disagreement.

"Sure, let's pray," I snapped back, and I was pretty sarcastic. "That's going to solve everything."

But in spite of my rather low opinion of the idea, we did kneel down and pray together. Dwight prayed first, because I really wasn't in a praying sort of mood. But by the time he got done praying, my heart was broken. And we learned something that day about praying together: when we ask God to help us understand each other's point of view, and pray for His help in resolving our differences, we're not mad at each other anymore.

On one beautiful snowy day Dwight and I were out taking a walk together even though it was 20 degrees below zero. The sun was shining, and we were hanging on to each others hands having a wonderful time. We did not even feel the cold. Until I said something, that is. At this point, I can't even remember what I said. But whatever it was, Dwight took it wrong. So he snapped right back. And within just a few seconds, we were both feeling pretty irritated. Pretty soon we dropped hands, and because Dwight normally walks faster than me, he was getting ahead. I really felt like Dwight needed to apologize. But I didn't think he would, because he was quite stubborn. All of a sudden I realized just how cold it was, not only outside, but on the inside as well.

I was having a real struggle within my heart at that moment.

"She started it, so she should apologize," I said to myself. And I had no intention of being the first to break the ice this time. But once again, that still small voice started working on my heart.

"What are you doing, Dwight?" I could almost hear it say.

"It's her turn to apologize, not mine," I stormed back. The Lord still tried speaking to my heart. "But Lord," I complained. "It seems like ever since I made the commitment to walk with You, I am always saying I'm sorry first. I thought this was a two-way street. It's just not fair. Aren't You working on her, too?" All of a sudden I thought of when Peter asked the Lord, "What about the others?" Christ told him to basically let Him take care of them.

"But you are the priest of the household, Dwight. How did you react when she said something that irritated you? Did you snap back at her, or did you do what Jesus would do?"

"But she's going to think I'm a wimp," I argued. "That I've really lost it now when I apologize first all the time."

"When you give your heart to Jesus, you aren't worried about self anymore," I seemed to hear. "You quit worrying about what people think, and do what is right." So I stopped in the snow and turned around and waited for her to catch up. I said, "Deb I am so sorry, will you forgive me?" At that very instant I could see tears shoot right off her cheeks.

"I am sorry also" I said. Even though it was twenty

degrees below zero, it is amazing how quickly you can warm back up. Then Dwight said, "Honey, let's pray right here." So we knelt and thanked God, right then and there in the middle of that snowy road, for working in our lives and teaching us that it is a sign of strength and growth—not weakness—to be able to say you're sorry and mean it.

When Dwight said, "Lord, forgive me for not being tender with my words. Help me learn to be a better husband. I am so sorry for treating my wife like this. Lord, I want to thank you so much for sending your Holy Spirit—that still small voice—to me and that I am beginning to obey, making practical the principles I already know. Because of Dwight's surrender, God spoke to me. It broke my heart in a way that might not have happened otherwise.

Although this seems like a small incident, it was a really important moment we both remember. There was a time in our relationship when we might have let things go on, all the while harboring unkind thoughts toward each other. Instead, we have learned to take care of it when God asks us to. Sometimes it is right away. Other times, it is when our hearts are subdued. In this particular instance, it would have been an awful cold walk home if we had not settled right then and there.

We have found praying together to be very helpful in our relationship, yet it is surprising how skittish many Christian couples become when you even mention the idea. Sadly, we've found that most husbands and wives, even Christians, don't pray together.

When you first get married, there is an initial excitement. But when that wears off many times spouses are just doing his or her thing, and there's not a real bond between them. But praise God, praying together can bring that back. Then when that happens, a marriage just gets better and better.

Can you start to see the effect of practical Christianity? We have the stories in the Bible for examples. We have Christ in the Bible, making the Word become flesh. In other words, He gave us that example and we need to follow Him. This is how the Bible becomes practical.

I was preaching a sermon about relationships to a very dedicated group of Christians. I asked the couples there to look at their spouse, and tell them they were sorry for whatever they had done wrong, to tell them that they loved them very much. Deb was sitting in the back, listening, and noticed the responses of those in the group. As I looked at the people sitting there, I was shocked at what I observed. I could hardly believe it! Some would not even look at each other. It was as if there was some kind of a barrier they just could not get past. Remember—these people were very dedicated Christians, the type who would let you know if you read out of another translation of the Bible other than the King James Version; the very ones who would remind you about the faults of others. Matthew 23:23 pretty much sums it up. "Woe unto, scribes and Pharisees, hypocrites! for ye pay tithe of mint and anise and cumin, and have omitted the weightier matters of the law, judgment, mercy, and faith: these ought ye to have done, and not to leave the other undone."

This used to be me. It is easy to hang on to the theory. We have got to remember that theory will not save us, nor will knowledge by itself. It is a practical living connection with Christ, not just theory, that we really need.

One thing I cannot stress enough about is time. We all have the same amount of time each day, twenty-four hours. Most of us, however, allow the clock to beat us instead of having us beat the clock. We never have the time to really sit down and think of what we are doing. We don't run our lives, life seems to always run us. Remember a few chapters ago I said that most people are so busy trying to make a living that they have no time to make any money. It really made me think. Are you one that says "I have no time to spend with my spouse. I have no time to spend with my children. I have no time to spend with God. This was the way it was for my wife and myself. I always said tomorrow, next week, next month or even I will have more time next year. Does this sound familiar?

Gems of Thought

From our experience it is a stark reality that unless you make the time tomorrow, next week, next month and next year it will never come. You need to realize that time is in control instead of you being in control of time. Deb and I found that when we started to take that time with God to listen and be still, our insurmountable problems began to have solutions.

35

Overcoming the Boogie-Man Blues

Fear was a problem that was big for Deb. Her biggest fear was someone breaking into our house. No matter how much I would try and reason with her I could not get past home plate. I would say things like "Deb, putting one more lock on the door won't help in the least little bit. If you put twenty locks on the door I could kick it open with about one to three kicks." I would tell her that doors are not very strong at the latches in fact that would be their weakest point. "Deb" I would continue, "even if they didn't come through the door they can knock a window out in a heartbeat." I would try to explain that there is no safety in mans devices. Try as I might I only made her more upset. She did not want to listen to me. To be honest she was actually putting her head in the sand so to speak. She would not be honest with herself. To her a lock had more safety than her guardian Angel.

Just before we made the move to our wilderness home in Montana we were told by a number of people to watch out for the Grizzly bears. Our children were ages 10, 5, and 4. It was a concern to us also about those big grizzlies. My wife especially was petrified of bears. "What are we going to do out there?" She would ask me. We had some advice from some of our close friends like "Make sure you wear bells and beat sticks together when you go outside. Another one was "whenever you go outside make sure you take a gun with you." Can you imagine I would say to my wife when we would get home to talk about these things teaching my children to pack a 357 magnum with them wherever they went. What are we going to do, never let our children go outside?

Our children were not afraid at all. They said mom and dad you and the teachers in our church say we have guardian angels that excel in strength. Is that true?

"Yes," we would tell them. "Well then God will take care of us," they said. Isn't it amazing that we teach our children truths from the Bible, but by our example we are telling them it is all just a fairy tale?

When I learned this lesson about fear in Montana , it felt like a huge mountain rolled off my back. I never knew it was so heavy!

While living in Michigan and Oklahoma, I had often been afraid. If I heard noises around the house, I would be fearful.

Of course, I didn't want the children to know this.

"There are angels around the house guarding us," I told them with a pasted smile. But while the words were easy to say, in my mind I wasn't so sure.

When we first considered moving to Montana, my fears escalated at the very thought. I realized that there were wild animals and even some pretty strange people out there in the "boonies." The police would never make it in time to deal with any number of problems that could arise.

I was afraid of the bears in Montana more than the people, because there were a lot of horror stories about bear attacks. I also worried about the mountain lions. When Dwight first told me there were mountain lions in Montana, I got out the encyclopedia and read about them. It told how mountain lions liked to sit up in a tree and pounce down on their prey. It sent a chill right down my spine, and the children had a few concerns, too.

"But children, they're not going to do that from pine trees," I told them when they wanted to know if a mountain lion might pounce on them. It probably wasn't a very good answer, but it was the only one I could think of at the moment.

My fear really started when I was a young teen sitting on my bed going through some papers. Suddenly I heard someone walking, making crunching noises in the snow. Then I heard the crunching stop right at my window. I knew someone was watching me. I was really frightened. The next morning we saw tracks coming to my window. When I got married, any time Dwight would be gone over night, I made sure the doors were locked and the lights were off so no one could see me. I would keep the flood lights on outside. I even put a dresser in front of my bedroom door.

As I started to have children I became more afraid. When it was only me, I felt I could hide or get away, but not with children!

There were so many cases where I'd play a game with my kids so they wouldn't know the fear Mommy really had. I'd tell them we would have a P.J. party in Mommy's room or a camping trip or a slumber party, whatever to make it fun. We would all be settled in my room by dark. I didn't sleep much when Dwight was gone, because I felt I needed to be on guard to listen and be ready to call the police in time—which I did, many times, only to find out it was a raccoon or a deer outside. I didn't have the privilege of getting help by a close neighbor—I lived back in the woods. And my theory was if someone is back in my neck of the woods they are here to do something bad to me or my children. All the time I was reassuring my children that our angels were watching over us and Jesus was taking good care of us. But my insides would be turning upside down with dreadful thoughts.

The Boogie-Man Blues

"Lord," I said, "I really want to give this fear to You. I simply can't take it with me." And in all honesty, I have to say that God really did take my fear away from me.

I remember one incident that helped me get over my fear. It happened when Seth was about four years old. I had asked him to sweep the mudroom, but he soon came racing into the kitchen with a rather exciting report.

"Momma, Momma, a bear was right here," Seth held up his hand about six inches away from his nose. At that moment I realized Seth must have opened the door and been nose to nose with the bear, who was evidently just outside.

"Seth, did you shut the door?" I tried to hide the uneasiness in my voice.

"Momma, the bear was right here!" Seth repeated, once again placing the palm of his hand right up in front of his face. But while it was terrifying to think that the bear had been "right here," I was even more frightened at the prospect that the bear might have come inside.

"Seth, did you shut the door?" This time it was impossible to hide the anxiety in my voice and written all over my face. I knew if he hadn't, that meant the bear was in the garage, on the other side of my kitchen door. And that was a bit too close.

"Well, yes, Momma," Seth looked at me so sweetly, as if trying to understand what my worry was all about. "You didn't want the bear in the house, did you?"

This whole incident really struck me. Here I had been, nearly frantic, while Seth, who had been eyeball to eyeball with this bear, wasn't afraid at all. And I started thinking that if I really trusted in Jesus, I didn't have to be afraid. Here I was teaching my children how God saved Daniel from the lion's den, and the three worthies from the fiery furnace—yet I was still overcome by fear myself. And I learned to trust God that way, in a way

I hadn't done before. I wanted to have the faith of a little child, like Seth; to not be afraid of the bears or any other danger, because Jesus is with me every step of the way.

This wasn't our only experience with bears in Montana.

"Momma, there's our bear," Natysha whispered to me one day. I looked to find the bear just across the yard, not more than a quick stone's throw away.

"Walk sideways and get to the house," I whispered a hurried order to the children. Just as the children reached the house, the brown bear started to look me over.

"Dwight!" I called, trying not to alarm the bear. Fortunately, Dwight heard. Within seconds he emerged from the mudroom, brandishing a broom and shouting at the top of his lungs. That was more than the frightened bear could take—she made a beeline right up a tree while I cut just as straight a path into the house. And it was strange how many times a bear would pop out of the woods just as soon as the children came inside. And I knew that bear had been right there watching my kids.

"It's OK, Mommy," the children would reassure me. "Our angels are watching over us." But while I nodded in agreement, in my heart I felt like the children had more faith than I did. We had a brown bear that used to come and visit us about three times a day. So many times when the children came in the house, I would say, "Why did you come in?"

"Oh, the bear is here," they would answer. I learned to have peace over this situation.

As we look back upon it now we see that there were a few principles that gave Deb the victory over this fear syndrome. We found out that our children's faith was such an inspiration to us. In their childlike faith, we observed one of the things we ourselves needed so badly. Quiet time was another key factor that gave Deb the victory. It was not just the reading but the listening to that still small voice. We know that everything we hear is not always from the Lord. Satan also gives us impressions. This is why God's word is paramount. The principles from the stories and parables of the Bible need to go along with that still small voice. John 10:1-5 says "My sheep hear My voice."

Many times this is where people fail. They might have their quiet time but fail to listen and obey His word. But Deb surrendered this fear to Him who is able to save to the uttermost. "Lord," she said "whatever it takes help me." Isn't it amazing how many times our Heavenly Father uses that which we are afraid of the most to bring the victory? In Deb's case He brought that bear to us every day for close to a year.

Gems of Thought

How many of us are scared of the boogie-man. It might not be fear of breaking in but there are many things—if we are honest with ourselves have to admit—we are afraid of. A few examples are:
- Afraid of the dark
- Afraid of someone breaking in to your home
- Afraid of your children or yourself getting hurt
- Afraid of failure
- Afraid of what people think of you
- Afraid of wild animals
- Afraid of heights
- Afraid of getting into an automobile accident.

These are only a few but they are real problems. We need to do what we can ourselves God has given us intelligence. The Bible says come let us reason together. For instance, when we moved out to the wilderness of Montana we told our children not to try to pet the bears or for that matter any of the wild animals. If they saw a bear leave it alone. You see God does expect us to do our part.

If you will take the time to evaluate your life, and see what boogie-man blues you have in your closet, and take these principles that we have just shared, you will be an overcomer just like us. I suggest that you write them down and pray about them now. Remember that perfect love casts out all fear (1 John 4:17, 18).

36

Miracle of the Dead Trees

When we moved to Montana we had enough money to last us for a while, but certainly not indefinitely. About 4 years after the move, the money started to run pretty low. I never worried much about money because Dwight usually came up with it somehow.

"I'll dig a ditch by hand if I have to," he always used to say. He had determined to provide for his family. In any case, at this point in time our money supply was getting low, and I do mean very low.

"You'd better buy that shovel," I told Dwight one day.

"Why?" Dwight thought I was joking.

"Because that's about how much money we have left—enough to buy a shovel," I replied. "And you need to start digging some ditches."

Now the 35 acres we owned had a number of dead trees on it. And when we first moved to Montana, we tried to find out about their value.

"They'll be good for firewood," we were told. "Other than that, they're not worth much."

John, one of our employees at Remnant Publications, had

called in a logger and done quite well.

"Maybe you should check into those dead trees," John told me. "They are worth more now than they were a few years ago, because the market is so good." So after praying about our financial situation, I decided to call the same logger and see if we could get some money from the fallen timber on our property. The logger came out to see us. His name was Enos, and he was a very dedicated Christian.

"I think I can get 5 semi-truck loads of wood from your dead trees," Enos told us. "I'll be happy to give you $3,750.00 up front." That meant $750.00 per load.

"Well, what if you get more?" I wanted to know.

"How much do you think is here?" Enos asked.

"I was hoping for about eight loads," I replied.

Enos shook his head. Having been in this business for years, he had a pretty good idea how many loads could be expected.

"I'd be surprised if you get that much," he told us. "For one thing, part of your property is swampy ground, and another part is a lake. So you'll do well if you have even 15 acres of woodland here. And remember, we are only taking the dead trees."

"Yes," I replied. "But what will happen if you get more than you projected?"

"I'll give you $750 per load," Enos promised. He also estimated that it would take his loggers about one week to remove the dead wood from our property.

Well, the loggers came as promised and worked on our property for a week. In the meantime, we were busy praying that they would find lots of trees. At the end of the week, I went out to check on their progress.

"We're just about done," they told me. "Just a little bit more to do, so we'll be back on Monday morning to finish the job."

We kept praying. Monday afternoon when I went out to check on their progress, the loggers informed me that they had found another stand of dead trees.

"Seems like we missed one," they told me. "We'll be back to

take that stand on Tuesday, and after that we'll be done." We kept praying, and Wednesday afternoon when I went to check, they told me the same story with a little extra added.

"Dwight, we just can't understand this," Enos said. "How many places can a dead tree hide? We just finished cutting over here, and then we find more dead trees over there, and on it goes."

And I went back to my house rejoicing that afternoon, because I knew God was at work. There was no way they could find that many dead trees on our property, and yet they just kept finding them. It reminded Deb and I of the widow in the Bible and her jar of oil (you can read the story in 2 Kings 4:1-7), or the widow whose barrel with meal was continually replenished during a terrible famine (you can read that story in 2 Kings 17:7-15).

To make a long story short, Enos and his men cut timber on our fifteen wooded acres for a full three weeks. They finally did quit, but not because they had run out of dead trees. The other customers were getting upset because Enos was two weeks behind schedule!

During those three weeks, I stood at the window and watched those loads going out with excitement building. Every day I talked to the loggers and they would say, "We just don't understand! Every day we come expecting to finish this job, and everyday we find more fallen timber!"

Now Dwight and I had set a non-expensive budget for ourselves. You can live pretty inexpensively when you are out of debt, and we figured we could live on $13,000 per year. And by the time the loggers were done on our property, we had not $3,750 or 5 loads as originally projected, but $13,500 worth of dead trees. That is 18 loads. Can you comprehend that? Those were dead trees on 15 or less acres. God made dead trees. That was a real miracle—to get all that money off of dead trees and have our woods cleaned up at the same time. We have never forgotten how God provided for us there. In fact, it was a real turning point in our lives because we realized that if God can make dead trees appear out of nowhere, He can do anything. Every time we get low on funds now and I start to worry Dwight always reminds me not to lose my faith and to "remember the dead trees."

The miracle of the dead trees was a real faithbuilding experience for us, because it was something incredible that we could watch, right in front of our eyes, everyday. Since that time, as I have studied and thought about faith, I have wondered why there is so little faith on this earth. We call ourselves Christians, and yet so many times we don't believe.

In Hebrews 11:1 we read that "faith is the substance of things hoped for, the evidence of things not seen" and in verse 6 we read without faith it is impossible to please God, for he who comes to God must believe that He is, and that He is a rewarder of those who diligently seek Him.

Gems of Thought

Following is an acronym, which has helped me as I have tried to better understand the concept of faith:

F - stands for full surrender. Those who have faith will surrender fully to Christ, by taking time to hear the still small voice, read the Bible, and make it practical in their lives. They will die to self daily as Paul did, for salvation comes one day at a time—not a week in advance.

A - stands for action. Once we fully surrender, we need to move and do whatever He has called us to do. When God calls us to study our Bible, He didn't say next month or tomorrow, He said, "Now is the accepted time, now is the day of salvation." We have to make decisions to do things now, for tomorrow is like a mirage. It is always in front of us. We need to make changes when God puts it in our hearts, even if that means saying "Lord, I don't know how I'm going to do this, but you have said now is the time and I make a decision to do it now." We have to take action.

I - stands for less of I. Not I, but Christ, be honored, loved exalted, as the old hymn goes. Many people think, "Christ and I are one—and I am the one." But Christ is the one, not us, and we have to make sure He is fully in our actions, not our selves.

T - stands for trust. A lot of people think they cannot do anything in the Christian life. Christ would not tell us to walk and then not give us the muscles to do it with. God has given us the talent to do things, but we need to stretch our minds and do what God has asked us to do. And the key is to trust. We have to trust God for that is an integral part of faith.

H - stands for heaven. And that is the victory. We can be a part of Christ's heavenly kingdom by surrendering our lives to His will. "Not by might, nor by power, but by my spirit saith the Lord of Hosts" (Zechariah 4:6).

37

One Change at a Time

"My, don't you girls look nice today!" the lady beamed. Then she turned and looked me over. "And doesn't Mommy look nice, too!"

I was pleasantly surprised. I had been to the grocery store many times with the girls, and none of the grandmotherly types had ever said this before.

I had just started to wear dresses instead of my normal sweatpants or jeans. I started to put this change in practice after a conversation I had with my mother a few months before. Our business had started to grow and Dwight was in contact more and more with professional people. I would see these people in the office at times, and at times he would bring them home and have me fix dinner for them. My mom thought that I, as a successful businessman's wife, should dress nicer.

"Deb, why don't you dress more nicely?" she asked.

"I look nice, Mom," I would reply. "I'm not a sloppy dresser, you know." After all, I wore matching sweat suits and nice-looking jeans.

"But you really could look nicer, Deb," she would say.

One Change at a Time

We went through variations of this conversation a number of times. One day, after she brought up the subject again, I got kind of ticked off about it.

"O.K., fine," I said rather sarcastically at the end of our conversation. "I will dress nicer."

So the next time I went out-which happened to be to the grocery store-I put on a nice casual dress.

"Well, if I'm going to look like this, I sure don't want to be alone," I thought to myself. So I put dresses on our two girls, also. It was a shock that first time when the lady said what she did. I fought with my conscience, trying to pass it off as a fluke. But the very next time we went to the store the same thing happened. I could hardly believe it! This time, however, the lady was with her husband.

"You know, it's sad," he chimed in. "Women just don't seem to look as nice anymore. And children, especially girls, only wear dresses for weddings, church, or maybe a funeral."

These types of comments continued to happen on a regular basis, as we wore dresses more and more. This made me think a lot about the way I looked. I kept asking myself, "Does the way I dress make that much difference?"

I also noticed that I felt more like a lady in a dress, and that people treated me more like a lady as well. You know, stockboys moved their boxes out of the way to let me go by and men held more doors open. It seemed like people gave me more respect, and I felt better about myself, too.

One day when I got home from the store, I actually forgot about changing and just left my dress on. When Dwight came home the first words that came out of his mouth were "Are you going somewhere?"

"Why?" I said, not catching on.

Learning to Walk With God

"Well, you've got a dress on and I never see you in a dress unless you are going to church. You look beautiful." That was it! I was convinced. This all happened about twenty years ago, and as we look back on it now, we see how God was leading me even though I didn't know it.

When Deb first decided to make the change it had nothing to do with Christian principle. Neither of us had a clue that there was even a hint in Scripture about dress. It wasn't long afterwards that I was at a religious meeting and heard some people arguing over what they should wear. Some were saying it matters what you wear while others were saying just the opposite. I went home to start a new study with nothing to prove on either side. Texts from the Bible started to come alive. Deuteronomy 22:5 was one of the first texts that I found. I also discovered other texts about modesty, simplicity, and doing whatever we do to the glory of God. It's amazing what you can find and learn when the heart is open. Deb and I started to realize that God has a people—a team—and He wants that team to shine forth as the noonday sun, to be an example and a testimony.

I also remembered seeing Dwight looking at a young lady one day as we were walking together. She had on the typical jeans and sweater. He kept looking at her until finally I said, "Dwight, why are you looking at her? Should I wear jeans?" "Not at all," he said. "Why then were you looking?" I asked. Dwight wasn't really sure. He started to think about it, and ask questions. "Do you look at any girls besides your wife?" he asked some of his friends. "It just depends," they would say. "Depends on what?" Dwight wanted to know. "If they are good looking?" "No, mainly if they have a nice figure," his friends would say. "If they wear clothes that show off their figure. You know, like tight-fitting clothes or a low-cut top." Then Dwight began to ask me some questions. "Why do you wear tight jeans or a low-cut top?" he wanted to know. "Do you dress that way so guys will look at you?" "Absolutely not!" I told him. "Then why?" he wanted to know. "I guess it's because it's the style," I told him. "I don't want all the guys looking at me."

I started doing some research and asking questions of more guys and girls. I found out that God created the man to be the aggressor. But the man has to have something to be aggressive with. Looks and smell are the things that get a guy started. For a girl it is touch. Do you start to get the picture? If a lady wears certain types of clothing it creates a certain type of reaction in men. It's just the way it is. Deb and I took time to figure this out and what a blessing it has been. I don't worry about all the guys looking at her anymore. She wants to reveal her beauty to me and me only. That doesn't mean she wears a burlap bag for a dress and a brown paper sack over her head. She looks nice but dresses simply and modestly.

I have come to learn that part of being a Christian lady is to dress to the glory of God, and not unnecessarily tempt men to look at me with a lustful heart. Since the time that I made my change twenty years ago, Dwight and I have been able to just sit down together and open up and listen to each other about how we see these things. What a balance God has given us in our spouses, if we would not fight with one another but learn from each other.

Gems of Thought

God has a plan for how we should eat, exercise, and treat each other, and the way we dress is no different. People will know by our fruits. The Holy Spirit started working on my mind that our dress makes a difference. You know a football player by the type of clothing he wears. It's the same in almost any other sport. It even goes further than that. All football teams don't wear the same color jerseys. You know them by their colors. God wants us to be set apart, not because we are better. God forbid! He sets us apart because He wants us to be able to be lights that can be seen to guide other people in the right path. I would like to interpret again what I have said before. The changes need to come from the inside out. But people see us from the outside in. That is why so many people are disappointed when they get to know a so-called Christian. It is also why so many Christians are absolutely miserable. They think changes on the outside alone will make them better Christians.

38

Being Faithful in Little Things

One of the things I really wanted God to do for me while I was in Montana was to increase my faith. More than anything else I wanted to live by faith, and I prayed for this often.

I got up very early on one particular morning, and prayed especially that God would help me to be faithful that day. By the end of my quiet time, during which I spent 30-45 minutes praying, I was impressed that God would answer that prayer. Of course, I had no clue what events might transpire that day. Only that I had asked God to keep me faithful, and felt His promise.

It was winter then, and the Montana snow was five feet deep on the level. I needed to cut wood that morning, for that's how we heated our house. So I picked up my chainsaw and gas can, and, with the aid of some snowshoes which kept me from sinking hip-deep in the snow, headed into the woods.

I was cutting dead trees that day—trees with black bark and an even darker blackish moss. It made quite a mess when the trees tumbled down. Before long, the entire clearing seemed to be covered with black flecks of moss and bark.

I cut for 30-45 minutes before running out of gas. Then I headed for where the gas can was safely stowed at the edge of the clearing. I put it there so it wouldn't be hit by a tree. I took the gas can back to my chain saw. When I finished filling the chainsaw, I put

201

the little black cap on the back of the gas can nozzle and took it back to the edge of the clearing. But after another 45 minutes of cutting when I went to get gas again, the gas cap was gone. I realized that the cap must have hit my leg when I took it back.

Now this might seem like a small thing to you, and in many ways, it was. A new gas cap wouldn't cost very much, although I'd have to drive 70 miles to get it. Even then, I wasn't sure if the nearest store would have only a lid. Of course, the expense of an entirely new gas can wouldn't have broken our budget either. But it was the principle of the thing that bothered me.

I didn't want gas sloshing out on me as I walked through the woods. I was also less than excited about driving so far for a cap. And it seemed so unnecessary to buy a new can just for the cap, when the other was perfectly good.

I turned and looked at the clearing where I had now been cutting for nearly two hours. It seemed like a sea of black specks, some bark and some moss, many of which were now stomped into the snow by my constant moving about.

"You'll never find that lid," I thought to myself. But I hate losing things, so I decided to try anyway. I'm a goal-oriented person, and I was intent on finding that lid. But the longer I looked, the more hopeless things seemed to get. After 20-25 minutes, I was so frustrated I was ready to quit.

"I hope I didn't step on it," I mumbled. "In that case it's somewhere down in this 5 feet of snow, and there's no way I'll ever find it."

It was then, when I felt so frustrated and was just about to give up, that I heard that still small voice speaking to my heart.

"Dwight, do you want me to help you find it?"

"I'm not going to bother the Lord with this little bitty gas cap," was the first thought that came into my mind. "That's ridiculous!"

That's when the Bible story of Naaman flashed into mind.

"If God had asked you for a big thing," the servants had reasoned with Naaman, "wouldn't you have done it? Why not do this little thing?"

Being Faithful in Little Things

And I wondered if that wasn't how God felt about me and my little bitty gas cap. It was only a little thing, yet surely He could and even would want to do it.

There was a struggle going on in my heart just then, over this super-small thing. That morning I had asked God to help me with my faith, yet here I was, not wanting to trust Him on such a trivial thing.

I'm happy to say that, in the end, God won out. I knelt right there in the snow and asked Him to help me.

"Lord, you've asked me to be faithful in that which is least," I told Him.

"You know where the gas cap is, and so do your guardian angels. It seems like such a small thing. But I'm asking you right now to help my unbelief so I can be more faithful. And I'm asking you, in the name of Jesus, to help me find the cap."

Then I thanked God in advance for helping me find it, for I did believe that He would.

When I got done praying, I stood up and looked around. Having been walking around for 25 minutes, I wasn't quite sure where to start. So I looked down, and there, sticking out as if it were fluorescent orange, was the gas cap only a foot from my feet!

I was so overjoyed, I could have jumped to the top of a tree! But I settled for thanking God for His help, and learning the lesson He had for me there. For through this experience, God was teaching me that He cares about the little details of my life.

Gems of Thought

As I look back on it now, I don't think I would ever have this faith-building episode if I hadn't spent time with God that morning. I asked God to work on my heart that day—to keep me faithful and be faithful to me—and He did.

I believe with all my heart that some of our prayers hit the ceiling because we don't take time with God in the morning. Because we don't build a relationship with God, then we pray and nothing seems to happen. I've learned through experience how important that relationship is, for when we have it, God can really work in our lives. As we continue to walk and grow even closer to God, He is eager to show that even the small stuff is really important to Him.

39

Where is Your Wilderness?

I wish I could say that our life in Montana was totally idyllic, but it really wasn't. And we did have a lot of things to work out. You know, in Michigan we really weren't together for that much of the day. But in Montana we were together all the time. We ate together, got on a schedule—even brushed our teeth together. And the kids loved it. They had both Mom and Dad around, and they liked the consistency of a schedule. Dwight got more and more involved with the children, and we did a lot of projects together around the house.

There was also a difference when it came to disciplining our children. If I had a problem with the children, Dwight would get off the ladder, or stop whatever else he was doing, and come help me deal with it.

After reading the majority of this book you know how much of a type A personality I am. When I made the commitment to help Deb with the children more, I did not realize what I was in for. Since before we had made the move I never was home that much and when I would get the chance to get a project done that I might have started I knew that I only had a few hours or at best a weekend day. When I would hear the kids start to complain or argue over something I would usually yell at Deb and tell her to take care of it. This was not because I didn't know how to handle it. I just did not think I had the time to mess with it. When we told our children to do something you can be sure that I didn't have to say it twice. Besides I would think, Deb will do just fine.

Learning to listen to that still small voice and then obey now no matter what, is not always very easy for me to do. On this particular day I was engrossed in my work. In fact I was about 35 feet above the ground on a scaffold. I was putting trim up and it was at the very top of the gable end of the house.

Now to make matters worse I was up there doing this job by myself. The scaffold was teetering back and forth and it was not a good situation. I was putting this last piece on at the very top and struggling more than just physically. Because it was not going too well I was already a little stressed. I had been talking to God to help me overcome my emotional feelings. Just then I heard a noise and it wasn't the noise of something falling. This noise was the noise of my children starting an argument.

The noise got louder and louder and I was saying to myself "where is Deb? Can't she hear this? I mean I am outside 35 feet up in the air. The doors are closed and I have no problem hearing them." I was just about ready to yell—since for years that had been my mode of getting attention—when I heard God's voice speak to my heart. Dwight you need to take care of this situation. "But Lord" I said Why can't she take care of it? Can't you see what I am doing way up hear? After I let my conscience be quiet for a minute that ever speaking still small voice said "Dwight don't ever forget why you are on this earth. It certainly is not to put this board up. You're here to develop a character after the pattern of my Son.

I want you in heaven so that we might spend eternity together. You must learn to obey with the motive of love another words from the inside out. When you do this you will be safe to save. The other reason and the only other is that you take time to train your children, especially by example, to be safe to save. Then you will be able to go out with power and be the light to the world that I want you to be. Your children are much more important than this board. I was so glad I listened. I first thanked God for His mercy and love to keep pursing me. Then I asked Him for wisdom to handle my children in a right spirit.

I climbed down off that scaffold, went into the house, and took care of the problem. As I was climbing back up I was so excited and so filled with peace that I had done my Lord's will. By the way, I did still finish the trim that day.

Of course, there were temptations to get too busy in Montana, too. After we had been there for a while Dwight bought a bulldozer and backhoe. Then he earned extra money punching roads for people, or helping them build a cabin. We got a mobile phone, and before we knew it, he was getting too busy again.

"Honey," I told him, "you are going to have to work on this. I am going to help. I will take the phone calls for you."

Dwight's friend Tom also saw the problem, and had some advice as well.

"When someone asks you to do something, don't say yes," Tom told Dwight. "Say 'I'll have to pray about that.'"

I could share many more stories of my wilderness experience with you. How God helped me to simplify my life, spend more time with Him. How He taught me to put him ahead of my business instead of my business ahead of God.

I am not saying I am perfect now, but during my wilderness experience I learned how to control time instead of letting it control me. And I learned so many other things.

If you are struggling with some of the same problems that I've had to deal with in my life, I pray that you'll seriously consider having a wilderness experience.

It doesn't have to be in Montana, or even in the wilderness.

But it does have to be in a quiet place, where you can slow down and make God first in your life.

Too many people are busy thinking, like I did, that somehow things will change by themselves. But I can tell you from experience, they never will.

If we want to make God first, last and best in our lives, we must "clear our slates" so to speak, to make and take time with God.

Jeremiah 29:13 says, "If with all your hearts ye truly seek me, ye shall ever truly find me, thus saith our God." "And you will seek me and find me, when you search for Me with all your heart."

If after reading this book you feel that you, too, need a wilderness experience, please don't put it off. The Israelites had to pass through the Wilderness before they reached the Promised Land, and the same is true for us today. May God help us each to travel that road, and surrender our lives to Him more fully with each passing day.

Gems of Thought

Isn't it something how we are always trying to justify our situation. It usually starts out with the word "but." My mom use to tell people that I was not the normal child when I first was learning how to speak. She said that most children would learn to say mommy or daddy but she said the first words out of my mouth were "But Mommy why?" Even though we may grow up selfish God is so patient with us. With me that day He was striving. I had been asking the Lord to help me listen no matter what. Now when He did just what I asked Him to do I did not like it in the least little bit. I am so glad He does not give up on us.

Do you want to have this walk that I am describing? You can. Kneel down right now and ask him who faileth not to show you what you need to do. Make the choice. Remember it is not usually the big things as much as the little things that trip us up.

40

How Has Christianity Changed Your Life?

Has being a Christian changed you into the likeness of Jesus? Or are you hypocritical, judgmental and miserable? Have you found that walk with God you are seeking? If not, what is the solution? In my seemingly short time on this earth, three principles have helped me to know what it means to walk with God. I can assure you that if you take these principles to heart, your life will change and others will see the changes in you.

Principle #1: Take the advice of Psalms 46:10, "Be still and know that I am God."

Many of us want to be holy, but we do not take the time. We might have read and even memorized much of the Bible and other inspired books and that is good. However, have you been "still" to know the God you read about?

Psalms 139:17,18 says, "How precious also are thy thoughts unto me, O God! How great is the sum of them! If I should count them, they are more in number than the sand: When I awake, I am still with thee."

Is God still with you when you get up in the morning? Remember He is our strength. I have found I must not begin the day without Him. When I say this, I'm not talking about a quick prayer in the morning, but I mean really taking time with Him-communion!

"Take time to be holy." Do you want to follow Jesus' example? He arose early in the morning when everything was quiet and still. "Awake my glory! Awake, lute and harp! I will awaken the dawn." Psalm 57:8.

Principle #2: When you pray and study, open your heart to God as you would to a friend. Ask like King David did for a contrite spirit—a full surrender.

Read the Bible as if God wrote it just for you. Ask yourself, "How does this apply to me for today? Remember, the Holy Spirit will teach you all things.

As this book describes, as I grew up all I could see were the "dos and don'ts." I didn't understand that because of God's love for me, He set me apart so I would be protected from the harm that is the natural result of disobedience. I didn't realize that His laws and statutes were for my well-being and happiness.

Did my experience with Christianity change me? Yes, I had just enough to give me one big headache! I had "just enough religion for a migraine." To put it simply, I was trying to conform to all the rules and regulations without a true conversion of the heart.

Brothers and sisters, let's be honest. Are you doing the same thing? If so, will you be honest and admit it? How has your experience as a Christian changed your life? Has it changed you just like it did me—just enough to make you unhappy and restless with your life? Or are you the "microscope" type of Christian, who scrutinizes most everybody and everything to point out their minutest flaws? I can assure you, either way is a nasty and most discouraging trap to be in. Do we have just enough religion to give us one big headache?

There are two different types of homes today, with many variations in between. On the one side is utter chaos, while the opposite is the picture of perfect harmony. Which picture depicts you and your family?

To be even more specific, do you talk about others in front of your children? Do you point out the faults of others, but continue to argue and fight with your spouse?

Dads, do you reprove your children for watching certain programs while your attention is fixed on the sports channel? Do you think Jesus would watch a football game, or any other sport? Can you imagine Jesus saying, "Man, did you see the way he got creamed at the line of scrimmage?"

Moms, do you tell your children to clean their rooms while yours is a mess? The questions could go on and on!

My wife and I have been there. Do you see how we can turn not only our children off, but our families, friends, and neighbors as well by saying we are Christians but not living what we believe?

Principal #3: Remember "He that is faithful in that which is least, will be faithful in that which is much" (Luke 16:10).

In these experiences that we have shared with you did you begin to realize it was the small daily trials that tripped us up? Again I can't over emphasize that to learn to walk with God is not some big profound challenge out there. If it was, then only certain people would succeed. This then would not be fair. Every one of us can improve our lives. Deb and I have shared these examples. First look at the things which lie nearest. For example if your car needs to be cleaned, clean it and keep it cleaned. The Christian world as a whole has missed the boat. We either come up with a bunch of rules and regulations or we just go to the opposite extreme and say "it doesn't matter what you do, just believe." Like me the world wants to see something better than they have. In the end it doesn't matter how smart we are, it matters how we have treated ourselves, our families, and even people we don't know.

Now, by God's grace, instead of grumbling about what I shouldn't eat, I first see Jesus as my Example. What did He do? Then I look into the Bible and search with an open heart to see what His love tells me, knowing that He reveals it for the same reason He hung on the cross for me—only for my wellbeing and because He loves me. Jesus says, "I am come that they might have life, and that they might have it more abundantly" (John 10:10).

If God were to open my eyes to some duty I had been neglecting by His grace, I wouldn't say, "Oh boy, just another rule; this has gone too far!" Instead, I would say, "Thank you, Lord, for your wisdom and love to tell me this. I know it's for my best. Do I have to wait until tomorrow Lord? Can I start now?"

When Peter truly knew Jesus, he didn't shrink from dying the way Jesus did. His only request was to be crucified upside down. Can you see the difference? The Bible says, "Come, let us reason together" (Isaiah 1:18).

How foolish—and I mean utterly foolish—can we be by saying it really doesn't matter what we eat, as long as our food isn't unclean! Or that it really doesn't matter what we watch on television? Even if it is a good program, is it robbing God of His time? Music and dress are other areas that we can get hung up on, or feel resentful about, and these are just a few.

That was my problem. I was always trying to justify my way of doing things. Friends, I took the wide path leading to destruction. I did my own thing. I had money, worldly pleasure, and everything else that the devil had to offer. Yet I still wasn't happy!

It was when I gave my heart fully to Jesus Christ, and said, "Lord, I am tired of having it my own way," that I began to understand the Scripture in a new way—just like Nicodemus did.

Please read the chapter on Nicodemus in the *Bible Study Companion Set*. It is in the book The Desire of Ages, pages 95-100. Read it prayerfully. It will explain what I have been trying to say.

Praise God, I asked for that eyesalve He freely offers! See Revelation 3:18. What a blessing it has been for my family and I! Now I see the do's and don'ts in an entirely different way. Now I realize that they are my protectors.

Friends, I don't mind being different anymore. I am thankful for 1 Peter 2:9, which says, "But you are a chosen generation, a royal priesthood, a holy nation, His own special people that you may proclaim the praises of Him who called you out of darkness into His marvelous light."

How Has Christianity Changed Your Life?

When we give ourselves fully to God, we have the privilege of walking with Him as Enoch did—not in a trance, but as we take care of our everyday duties. Then we will live what we say we believe. Only as we fully commit our lives to the Life-giver can He impart to us a sweet rest and peace of mind.

Yes, now I can truly say that being a Christian has changed my life! I love now what I used to hate, and I see more clearly what used to be obscure and dreary.

Because of this change, people are coming up not only to me, but also to my wife and children. The very questions that Deb and I argued over are the same questions we now get asked. Friends, it is our lifestyle, not our office in life that has the greatest influence on others.

Our children have been asked, "Don't you think your parents are too strict because you don't watch television? Why are you having school at home? Why can't you eat between meals? Don't you feel cheated because you can't listen to contemporary Christian music?" And their answer is "No, we don't even miss it!" They know they have chosen a better way of life.

As you begin to have a real relationship with Jesus Christ, our great Example, you will truly see that being different from the world, and maybe even from other Christians, is not legalism or a curse. You will see that being different is a blessing! It is, quite simply, a sign of God's protecting love.

Gems of Thought

Today I am thankful that being a Christian really has changed my life. And if it hasn't already, it can change your life too! But time is so short—don't put this off for one more day. As the Bible says, "Now is accepted hour, now is the day of salvation" (A paraphrase of 2 Corinthians 6:2). Drop to your knees and truly give Jesus your whole heart. Ask Him with an open mind, "What must I do to be saved?" Take time to hear that still small voice. As you do, you will see how to walk with God.

213

Epilogue

Many things have happened in our lives since Deb and I finally made that full commitment to God. Our oldest daughter, Alysha, is married with a life of her own, and Natysha and Seth will soon be next. While we don't regret the fact that our children are growing up, we also know that until that happens, they will continue to fill the uppermost part of our minds and activities.

In 1985 we founded Remnant Publications, a printing ministry dedicated to sharing the set of life-changing books that have meant so much to us in our walk with God. This set of books, which we call *The Bible Study Companion Set*, helps people understand the Bible in simple and practical ways. Since 1985, Remnant Publications has placed literally millions of these life-changing books in the hands of those who otherwise would not have received them.

We moved out to Montana for a wilderness experience, to get close to God and allow Him to lead in our lives. We loved our life in Montana, because it brought us so much closer as a family. But after about seven years in Montana, we felt God calling us back to Michigan. The 40,000-square-foot building from Trailmaster never sold, and we felt God could use it for Remnant.

It wasn't easy to move back, yet we felt God was calling us to do another work for Him. When we gave up our peaceful Montana lifestyle, it would have been easy to lose our day-by-day walk with God. But we brought back some important principles from our "wilderness experience"—principles that have helped us keep that all-important relationship alive. I've shared those life-changing principles in this book, and believe with all my heart that they are the keys to true success.

One of those principles, that of spending time with our family, is still very vital to me. Even when we have had a tough day we make time to sit down and just talk with one another. It continues to keep us bonded together. My family is still the most important responsibility I have.

The importance of doing things right away—as God leads you—is another important principle I hope you've seen in this book. Some people think that when they get it all together, build their business, have kids or make a lot of money—then they will take time to serve God. And I used to think this way.

A third principle—and the one I'd like to leave you with—Is the importance of having a day-by-day, moment-by-moment surrender to God. Deb and I have learned by experience that it's easier to accomplish one little goal—like turning off your TV set for a month—than it is to make permanent lifestyle changes. It's so easy to slip back into a rut. Maintaining a moment-by-moment surrender to God on an ongoing basis, like any other major lifestyle change, can be a real challenge.

We see this principle in action all the time in the fitness center our family also owns and operates, "A Better Way of Life." When we share the principles of successful weight loss with our customers, many of them get very excited about their program. They start off with a vigor that few can match! Unfortunately, the enthusiasm begins to wear off after two or three weeks. We see some of them less and less, until finally they quit altogether.

Others do one part of the program well, but think the rest is too much to ask. For example, they may exercise vigorously but refuse to change their diet. Or vice versa. I have personally seen a number of members work out consistently for a year and not lose a pound. That's because it takes all—a full surrender to the whole

215

program—to really lose weight. To change a habit is one thing, but to make that habit a lifestyle—now that is the golden key.

When things get busy, it's easy to lose our walk with God. I have to admit that keeping a balance in my life—even when working for God—has been a challenge. I've had to relearn some things I thought I already knew, but God has been with us every step of the way. It seems as though most of us work for God but fail to walk with God. That's been a challenge with the "busy-ness" of it all, but God has been faithful.

I pray that you have been blessed by the practical ideas inside this book, but even more than that, I pray that you—if you have not done so already—will take up your God-given responsibilities and start where you are. Remember you are only a failure when you quit. The bottom line is don't put it off. You too, can have, "A Better Way of Life."

"Learning to stay with God"—that's the next step you take after "Learning to walk with God." By His grace, that's exactly what Deb and I have determined to do—and it's also what my next book will be all about.

For more information concerning speaking engagements
or purchasing books in quantity.
Please write to:

c/o Dwight Hall
Remnant Publications
649 E. Chicago Rd.
Coldwater, MI 49036

You can also reach us via:
Phone: (517) 279-1304
E-mail: dwhall@charter.net
Web: www.remnant.info